The Palestinian-Israeli Impasse: Has U.S. Policy Run its Course?

Proceedings of the Tenth Annual
Center for Policy Analysis on Palestine
Conference

The Center for Policy Analysis on Palestine
Washington, DC

February 2002

The views, facts, and interpretations presented in these papers are those of the authors and speakers. They do not necessarily reflect the views of the Center for Policy Analysis on Palestine or The Jerusalem Fund. The material may be used without permission, but with proper attribution to the Center for Policy Analysis on Palestine.

The Palestinian-Israeli Impasse: Has U.S. Policy Run its Course?

© 2002 by The Jerusalem Fund for Education and Community Development
Printed in the United States of America
ISBN: 1931518408
Library of Congress Control Number: 2002100954

The Center for Policy Analysis on Palestine
2425-35 Virginia Avenue, NW
Washington, DC 20037
Phone: (202) 338-1290
Fax: (202) 333-7742
E-mail: info@palestinecenter.org
Website: www.palestinecenter.org

Contents

International and Grassroots Initiatives

Where Do We Go from Here: Palestinian and American Perspectives

Preface

On 2 November 2001, the Center for Policy Analysis on Palestine (CPAP) held its annual conference, "The Palestinian-Israeli Impasse: Has U.S. Policy Run its Course?" For its tenth anniversary, the Center presented a critical appraisal of U.S. policy in the Middle East and Central Asia, with special focus in the Palestinian-Israeli conflict. It is this long-running conflict that is central to the understanding of how the United States is perceived in the Arab world, the Muslim world, and beyond.

The tragedy that struck the United States on 11 September 2001 underscored the urgent need for a realistic assessment of U.S. policy toward the Middle East. We are especially proud to have gathered together speakers internationally recognized for their insight and experience to address issues that will have a significant impact on America's future relationships with the countries and peoples of this vital region of the world.

Their presentations are collected in this volume. With its publication, the Center continues to enhance public awareness of the impact and implications of U.S. policy and to inform the public debate underway in Washington and abroad.

This volume will serve as a valuable resource for those seeking to understand the reasons, the context, and the environment that led us to the situation we face post-11 September.

Introduction

The tenth annual Center for Policy Analysis on Palestine (CPAP) conference was still in the planning stages, and experts on the Israeli-Palestinian conflict had already been invited to speak, when the tragic events of 11 September unfolded. Although the emphasis was shifted by those events, the conference took place with a renewed sense of purpose and urgency.

Ambassador David Satterfield delivered the opening remarks, "The Palestinian-Israeli Impasse: Is There a Way Back?" He began by emphasizing that "the events of 11 September, like the Gulf War in 1990 and 1991, have not changed the fundamental realities of the peace process." According to Satterfield, there is still "a fundamental interest … on the part of Israel and the Palestinians in finding a way back from violence, a way back from threats, a way back from provocation and escalation, and into a direct dialogue that yields for each side those things that are most important to them and can ultimately create once more an environment for negotiation."

U.S. Policy and the Palestinians

The first panel, moderated by Naseer Aruri, professor emeritus, University of Massachusetts at Dartmouth, discussed "U.S. Policy and the Palestinians."

Former CIA Political Analyst Kathleen Christison addressed the roughly continuous U.S. policy on issues pertaining to Israeli-Palestinian relations through successive U.S. administrations. In fact, the present Bush administration includes officials and advisers from both the previous Bush and the Reagan administrations who "viewed Israel as a vital strategic bastion against Soviet advances in the Middle East and regarded the Palestinians as tools of the Soviet Union." They are now advocating a broad-based military campaign and "trying to build a case against Iraq" in the current struggle for control of the war on terrorism, according to Christison. The current administration's approach to terrorism is rooted in the belief that "there are no root causes for the terrorism—no legitimate grievances against Israel for its treatment of the Palestinians, no legitimate grievances against the United States for its support for Israel's actions, or for its sanctions against Iraq, or for its assertion of economic and political and military hegemony throughout the Muslim world. If you can write off bin Laden and *al-Qaeda* as causeless fanatics, you are relieved of any obligation to address causes, and Israel is let off the hook."

Professor Emeritus of Finance at the Wharton School of the University of Pennsylvania Edward Herman described the American media's role in fostering positive views of Israelis and negative views of Palestinians. Herman stated that in media coverage of the second *intifada* rarely, if ever, conveys the actual conditions on the ground endured by Palestinians on a daily basis. References to "violence" mean "stone throwing and shooting," and never refer to the "structural violence" of the Israelis, including "expropriating land, evicting people from their houses and demolishing them, seizing and diverting water resources." In the media, only Israel "responds and retaliates." When Palestinians kill Israeli leaders, it is designated as "terrorism." When Israelis kill Palestinian leaders, it is called "assassinating terrorists."

Princeton University Professor of International Law and Practice Richard Falk discussed "Humanitarian Law and U.S. Foreign Policy," from the perspective of using the events of 11 September as a stimulus for a critical examination of U.S. policies *vis-à-vis* the Israeli-Palestinian conflict, utilizing humanitarian and international law. Israel, according to Falk, has put pressure on the United States to ensure that the signatories to the Geneva Convention not meet on the issue of the Palestinians. The Palestinian leadership "have acquiesced to unreasonable conditions," and Israel has been able to "create facts on the ground." Falk noted that the United States bears a "huge responsibility for cynical manipulation of human rights law."

U.S. Policy in the Middle East and Central Asia

Edmund Ghareeb, professor of Middle Eastern history and politics at American University in Washington, DC, moderated a panel on "U.S. Policy in the Middle East and Central Asia."

Former CIA Political Officer Martha Kessler examined current relations between the United States and Syria. "U.S.-Syrian relations have had a discontinuous quality to them, jolted episodically by revitalized interest in the Arab-Israeli conflict and resolving it, and by our concerns over terrorism," according to Kessler. Syria has worked to promote a more peripheral role in its relationship with the United States, preferring instead to engage with the Europeans. Unfortunately, the United States has had its views on Syria largely shaped by Israel and other detractors.

Former UN Arms Inspector Scott Ritter discussed the root causes of terrorism, stating that "people are not born to commit crimes" or "to commit acts of terror." In order to discover the motives of terror one must ask, "what is it about America's policies that compels people to evolve towards terror, evolve towards committing crimes which, when one considers the peaceful character of the Islamic religion, fly in the face of the very cause these criminals purport to support?" Ritter explained that resentment in many parts of the world toward the United States is fostered by "America's unilateral policy objectives," which "always take precedence over the international community's policy objectives." "International law will be manipulated, abused, and indeed violated, when it suits America's unilateral policy objectives."

Professor Glynn Wood of the Monterey Institute of International Studies recounted the last several decades' in Afghanistan, and the current situation. When the U.S. intervention in the region began, Pakistan was in desperate straits as a result of the sanctions in the wake of their 1998 nuclear tests, and having a military dictator in charge. After the attacks on the United States, Pakistan discovered that all of a sudden they were made an offer they could not refuse, according to Wood. Pakistan accepted the U.S. request for support in its war, and provided "intelligence sharing, logistical support, and the use of Pakistani air space."

Marwan Bishara, research fellow at the Paris-based Le Centre Indisciplinaire de Recherches sur la Paix et d'etudes Strategiques (CIPRES), discussed the nature of the wars fought by the United States against the *al-Qaeda* terrorists and by

Israel against the Palestinians. The end of the Cold War seems to have marked the end of symmetrical conflicts involving the United States. According to Bishara, the new danger to American national security and interests is asymmetric warfare, "which would be fought against an 'opponent who might have a non-nation-state base, such as an ideology or religion'." Since 11 September "America has felt asymmetry." The problem with this asymmetry is that "bin Laden is not accountable as a state, [he] is an individual, and is hiding, and asymmetrical people don't fight fairly." Bishara stated there seemed to be a sense that the "Israelis felt vindicated" after 11 September, and they felt "the United States is going to be facing the same challenges that Israel has been facing ... [w]hen one hears Bush nowadays, it becomes clear that America's strategy is heading towards asymmetric warfare along the lines of the Israeli model, even though Israel's strategy has failed in Palestine."

International and Grassroots Initiatives

A panel on "International and Grassroots Initiatives" was moderated by Samih Farsoun, former Chairman of the Sociology Department at American University.

Alexandros Karides, Middle East Affairs program associate with the World Council of Churches (WCC), discussed "The International Ecumenical Response to the Palestinian-Israeli Conflict." Since 1995, the WCC has "placed a particular focus on Jerusalem's place in the final stage of negotiations and has called for it to be recognized as a shared city for three faiths and two peoples." At the start of the second *intifada*, "the patriarchs and heads of the Christian communities in Jerusalem denounced the aggression ... and affirmed their solidarity with the Palestinian people—Muslims and Christians alike—in defending the fundamental right to worship and prayer in Jerusalem."

Phyllis Bennis, Fellow at the Institute for Policy Studies, discussed the possibilities for Israeli-Palestinian peace in the wake of 11 September and whether, in the current environment, a breakthrough is possible. In working to achieve peace between Israel and the Palestinians, all of us are in "a moment when we cannot afford illusions." While the dialogue for justice for the Palestinian people matters in communities and on college campuses, so far it has had little effect "when engaging with power." Bennis pointed out that "final status issues alone will [not] motivate the public to support the Palestinians." Activists must say "we are supporting occupation and it is violating human rights," and "U.S. [made] helicopter gun-ships are attacking Palestinian civilians." It must also be emphasized that many in the region hate the United States, not "for who we are, but because after Israel bombs [the Palestinians] the parts say 'made in the USA'."

Executive Director of the Middle East Children's Alliance (MECA) Barbara Lubin discussed her activities as an activist for peace and justice. Addressing what has happened in the United States since 11 September, Lubin said, "I was not surprised that it happened," only that "it took so long to happen." Just prior to 11 September, she attended the International Conference against Racism in Durban, South Africa. At a rally during the conference she saw people holding signs condemning Israel's practices against the Palestinians, giving a "general feeling of people from all over the world … that Israel has got to stop its tactics."

Gila Svirsky, co-founder of the Coalition of Women for a Just Peace, discussed her work as an Israeli peace activist. One of the central problems the peace movement in Israel faces is that "the Israeli media ignore us, and therefore the world media ignore us." Even though it often "feels like a blackout of our message" is occurring, "little by little, over time, the Israeli grassroots peace movement has had an impact on Israeli attitudes and policies." This has been accomplished, in part, "by affecting American policymakers, institutions, and individuals … Israel is vulnerable to international pressure, particularly by the U.S. government." Whenever the United States decides to exert its influence on the concept of a just settlement, "the Israeli government would have to fall in line if the United States insists."

Kumi Naidoo, of the South African NGO Coalition, provided insight into his participation in the struggle against apartheid in South Africa, an experience relevant to the current Palestinian struggle for freedom. Comparing the South African and Palestinian experience, Naidoo observed that, "South Africa faced a moment exactly like this, where change seemed to be somewhere, but we always assumed that it would never come in our lifetimes. That, in fact, if it were going to happen, it would happen, optimistically, ten or maybe thirty or forty years later. But a deal was made far away from South Africa, and suddenly it happened." The catalyst for change in South Africa turned out to be Edward Shevardnadze, then Soviet foreign minister. "If you look at the history of how the political forces played out, how economic interests played in, how the cold war dialogue was happening, and so on, it was a deal that was done far away from our shores that actually had, in a sense, the decisive effect."

Where Do We Go from Here: U.S. and Palestinian Perspectives

The concluding session, "Where Do We Go from Here: U.S. and Palestinian Perspectives," was moderated by Center for Policy Analysis on Palestine Chairman Dr. Hisham Sharabi.

Dr. John Duke Anthony, president and CEO of the National Council on U.S.-Arab Relations, discussed the state of U.S. relations with the Middle East in the post-11 September climate, and the duties of the United States in that relationship. Without a comprehensive peace between Israelis and Palestinians, "American interests will continue to suffer heavy blows." U.S. action and inaction on the issue "is much more embedded in what has spawned and sustained terrorism than many appear willing to recognize." Anthony argued that the United States "does the American, Arab, and Israeli people no favor by refusing to assume the mantle of responsibility" in working to settle the Israeli-Palestinian conflict. He concluded by paraphrasing Edmund Burke, saying "all that is necessary for systematic and institutionalized suppression and injustice to prevail, and in this case, for relentless anger and acts of terror against Americans, Arabs, and Israelis to continue, is that enough good people do nothing."

President of the Union of Palestinian Medical Relief Committees Dr. Mustafa Barghouthi discussed the current situation on the ground in Palestine in remarks delivered via telephone from his home in Ramallah, the West Bank. He began by describing the situation in Ramallah, stating that "we are literally surrounded by tanks," and are "under complete siege." These acts are "unprecedented, even in any other previous occupation." The "process of collective punishment" has transformed the West Bank and Gaza Strip "into 220 clusters of prisons." But there is still cause for hope. The fact that the world is now realizing that the United States' goals in the region depend upon a resolution to the Israeli-Palestinian conflict "provides us with an opportunity to find a solution and a resolution" observed Barghouthi.

Taking place at a critical juncture in U.S. Middle East policy, the conference addressed issues crucial to American interests. By articulating the exigency of a reconsideration of U.S. policy, the speakers have provided the tools required to get past the events of 11 September, and to move toward a real solution.

The Palestinian-Israeli Conflict: Opening Remarks

by Hisham Sharabi

In its first ten years, the Center for Policy Analysis on Palestine (CPAP) has developed into one of the most important sources of analysis and discussion of issues involved in the Arab-Israeli conflict and the Palestinian-Israeli peace process. Since its founding in 1991, the Center has informed the political discourse in Washington and abroad regarding the American relationship to the Middle East and the Palestinian question. It has served as a forum for a wide spectrum of views, hosting speakers from within the Occupied Territories and Israel, U.S. administration officials, academics, journalists, and premier Arab and world statesmen. Despite the surrounding gloom we look forward to another decade of growth and service with hope and confidence.

The question before us this morning is whether U.S. policy in the Middle East has run its course, and with this, the implicit question as to whether the Bush administration will come up with an alternative policy in dealing with the unprecedented crisis we now face.

We are told that the administration does have a new initiative on the Middle East, including guidelines for a final status agreement between Israel and the Palestinians. On the other hand, we understand, following Mr. Peres' recent visit to Washington, that there is no such plan. According to *Ha'aretz* (26 October 2001), Mr. Peres was assured by senior U.S. officials that the Bush Administration had "no detailed plan on the Palestinian-Israeli conflict, but only general ideas, such as the vision of a Palestinian state," and that what Washington wanted most was "to return the situation to the way it was before the assassination [of the Israeli Cabinet Minister Rehavam Ze'evi] and to discuss ways to implement the Tenet understanding and the Mitchell Report." But more ominously, according to the *Ha'aretz* report, the Israeli visitors were told the following: "Washington is continuing to carefully monitor Syria and Iran, and in coming days, new names will be added to the list of terrorist organizations and wanted terrorists," and "anyone on the new list will be those fighting against Israel, such as members of Hezbollah."

Of course, the *Ha'aretz* report may not fully reflect the entire position of the Bush Administration. However, if the administration were genuinely committed to a new initiative, such an initiative would necessarily have to be rooted in the objective givens of international law, UN resolutions, and the agreements already reached between the two sides. But it is not really a new initiative that is required at this critical moment. What is required, rather, is a determination by the Bush Administration to uphold in a consistent and coherent manner past U.S. commitments on the central issues of the Arab-Israeli conflict: on withdrawal from the West Bank and Gaza, on dismantling the Jewish settlements, on recognizing the rights of the Palestinian refugees and the right of the Palestinian people to a viable independent state, and on Jerusalem.

What is urgently needed right now, before the window of opportunity closes shut again, is not abstract talk about a Palestinian state—significant as such talk may be—but rather, as Polly Toynbee of the *Guardian* put it (24 October 2001), what is needed is "the same thunderous and threatening language the President applied to the war in Afghanistan ... announcing an end to the double standards of the West's treatment of the Palestinians."

Chairman of the Center for Policy Analysis on Palestine Hisham Sharabi is professor emeritus of European intellectual history and Omar al-Mukhtar professor of Arab culture at Georgetown University in Washington, DC. He is the author of sixteen books and numerous articles, monographs, and conference papers. He has served as editor of the English-language quarterly Journal of Palestine Studies *for 28 years.*

The Palestinian-Israeli Impasse:
Is There a Way Back?

by Ambassador David Satterfield

I was intrigued by the title of this conference, "The Palestinian-Israeli Impasse"—there is certainly no doubt that the situation merits the word "impasse"—but then the following clause: "Has U.S. Policy Run its Course?" While the temptation would be to say yes, that of course is not our position.

But I would turn the clause around: "The Palestinian-Israeli Impasse or Crisis: Is There a Way Back?" It is more than a question of policy. Policy implies that there is some formulation, some intervention, some expression of will, desire, or intent by an outside party, whether the United States or others, that is the critical element to ending this very terrible, very threatening, very dangerous situation.

I would argue that third-party vision, presence, and will is certainly of grave importance—has been in the past, is now, and will continue to be—in helping to advance what we and others believe is strongly in our interest, as well as the parties'. That is of course a just, comprehensive, and lasting settlement not only on the Palestinian-Israeli track, but also on the Syrian and Lebanese tracks as well. But more important than that is the will, the courage, the determination of the directly involved parties to see such an outcome worked towards and ultimately achieved.

The crisis we face today—the impasse we are discussing—is very real. The human suffering on both sides has been terrible, loss of life, devastation of the Palestinian economy. But beyond these human, quantifiable tolls, I would identify for you, in my view, a far worse toll, and a far more lasting, more pernicious, and poisonous outcome. It is the loss of hope, of trust, and of confidence that through negotiation, however painful, however incremental and difficult, but through negotiation a process exists which can lead to a different kind of life for Israelis and Palestinians separately and together. That hope, that trust, and that confidence in a different kind of future was what motivated the parties before Oslo, made Oslo possible, and sustained the process known as Oslo during the mid-1990s. And it is that sense of confidence, trust, shared objectives, and above all, an operational working partnership—not love, not embrace, but a working partnership, a sense of a win-win or lose-lose proposition—that has been lost and which must be regained.

Twenty years ago, Anwar Sadat died. Six years ago, Yitzhak Rabin lost his life. Both men displayed courage, fortitude, and determination in the face of extremely difficult circumstances based on their convictions—earned through years of trying the alternatives—that only negotiation, a reaching out, establishing, and sustaining a partnership, could work to meet the long-term needs of Israelis to enjoy what has been called "the quiet miracle of a normal life." Only a partnership will allow the Palestinian people to realize their national aspirations and their right to live that same quiet, normal life as Palestinians.

Ten years ago, the Madrid conference opened a new world, we hoped, of hope, of trust, and of confidence. It was not based on external intervention. It was not based on a dictate coming from the United States or from anyone else. While the events of the Gulf War helped focus, sharpen, and shape regional views and the views of the critical parties concerned, what made Madrid possible—indeed, what made the first Camp David possible, what made Yitzhak Rabin and Shimon Peres' moves at Oslo and after possible—was the recognition by the parties themselves that they had no alternative to moving forward together. That sense, I fear, is in grave jeopardy, if not lost, and it must be brought back.

How to do it? There is certainly a crying need now for courage and leadership on both sides—leadership from the Israeli government in recognizing that lasting security can only be achieved through a process of political dialogue and negotiation leading to a lasting and sustainable settlement that meets basic Palestinian needs, as well as basic Israeli needs. It requires leadership and courage from Chairman Arafat and the Palestinian Authority (PA) to recognize that through violence, whether intentional or violence that others are allowed to pursue, the interests of the Palestinian people cannot be advanced. Continued violence will lead only to greater, more sustained, more devastating suffering, and a further steady decay in those forces that want to see peace, rather than those who see peace as threatening to their interests, to their darker vision.

It is important that leaders on both sides recognize that, like their predecessors in this peace process that has gone on for so many years, there really is no alternative except to reach out to each other on a basis of trust, confidence, and a sense that the best goals are advanced when both win. The alternative is that both lose. This is not a zero-sum game, and cannot be a zero-sum game if it is to succeed.

What is the role of the United States? What is the role of the international community in all this? Well, it must be to nurture, to facilitate, to sustain, and to encourage this process. But we cannot substitute for courage, determination, and vision by the parties themselves. That has been true throughout this process. We cannot be the object of their negotiations. They must be the parties and the partners in this process. We can be there. We can suggest. We can help move forward a process that runs into difficulties. This was the role we played in the most successful portions of the Oslo process in the mid-1990s. But at that moment, I would note, it was the parties themselves who worked out their agreements. They were far more successful at doing that than when we were put in the role of directly negotiating agreements. That was not a very successful formulation, and it would not be a successful formulation today.

The events of 11 September, like the Gulf War in 1990 and 1991, have not changed the fundamental realities of the peace process, the Israeli-Palestinian issue. There is still—there was before 11 September and remains after 11 September—a fundamental interest, we believe, on the part of Israel and the Palestinians in finding a way back from violence, a way back from threats, a way back from provocation and escalation, and into a direct dialogue that yields for each side those things that are most important to them and can ultimately create once more an environment for negotiation. There is a strong U.S. interest—there was before 11 September and remains after 11 September—in seeing this happen. What 11 September has done is to sharpen the focus, increase the importance and significance of such progress, and increase the harm done by a continuation of this poisonous, corrosive violence and loss of trust. It has not changed the fundamental equations. The United States remains engaged with the sides and will continue to be engaged with the sides in doing what we can to change this very, very difficult reality.

Has policy reached an impasse? No. We continue to look at ways in which we can work with the sides and, more importantly, bring the sides themselves together again to work out their difficulties. If there are things that we can do, we will. But the leadership required must come from them. We cannot replace that. Our role is to help. Our role is to facilitate what they are doing and to encourage them along. In the end, they must live with the reality of their decisions or failure to take decisions. We believe it is a very negative reality that exists on the ground today. It has to be changed. The parties themselves, however, must rise to the challenge of taking those very courageous, admittedly very difficult, steps. They will find the United States a partner. They will find the United States a presence with them as they move. But the movement, in the end, must be theirs.

 *David M. Satterfield was U.S. Ambassador to the Republic of Lebanon, Director of the Office of Israel and Arab-Israeli Affairs, and served in overseas postings in Saudi Arabia, Tunisia, and Syria. He also worked in the Bureaus of Near Eastern Affairs, East Asian and Pacific Affairs, and Intelligence and Research in Washington. From 1993-96, Ambassador Satterfield served as director for the Executive Secretariat staff and for Near East and South Asian Affairs on the National Security Council. He is the recipient of several Department individual and group Superior Honor awards, notably for his work on the Middle East peace process.*

U.S. Policy
And the Palestinians

Kathleen Christison
former CIA Political Analyst

Edward Herman
Professor Emeritus of Finance
Wharton School, University of Pennsylvania

Richard Falk
Professor of International Law and Practice
Princeton University

Perceptions of Palestine:
U.S. Middle East Policy

by Kathleen Christison

There is an old aphorism that says, "the apple never falls far from the tree"—meaning, of course, that the son never deviates very far from what he learned at his father's knee—and meaning, in the context we are dealing with here today, that President George W. Bush is very much like his father President George H.W. Bush, as a man and as a policymaker. This raises some very interesting issues, because if you judge by the people he has surrounded himself with, this apple actually fell from two trees: his father's tree and Ronald Reagan's tree. These are two very different trees, when you are talking about the Palestinian-Israeli situation. And this difference makes it difficult to discern not only where Bush and his policymakers are coming from, but also where they are going from here.

So I would like to discuss the whole issue of continuity in foreign policymaking as it concerns the Palestinian-Israeli conflict—whether there *is* continuity in fact, what differences there are from administration to administration, and what impact public impressions and perceptions have on the formulation of policy—ending up with some coherent picture of how we got to where we are today, of how U.S. policy has evolved to the point where it is today.

Let me go back to the point about President Bush falling from two different trees. As everyone knows, many of his principal policymakers are holdovers from the Bush Senior administration: Vice President Cheney, Secretary Powell, Condoleeza Rice. These are for the most part pragmatists, at least relatively speaking, like President Bush Senior himself—not friends of the Palestinians by any means, but also not overly inclined to tilt toward Israel.

But what is less noticeable is how many of those who had an influence on the Reagan administration's Arab-Israeli policy are back again, either in policymaking roles or hovering around the edges: Richard Perle, John Bolton at the State Department, Douglas Feith at Defense, Elliot Abrams on the National Security Council staff, Jeane Kirkpatrick, Frank Gaffney. These are some of the leading figures from a group of so-called neo-conservatives who played a large and prominent role in directing Reagan administration policy along the very strongly pro-Israeli and the decidedly anti-Palestinian lines that it followed throughout its eight years.

During the Cold War, the neo-conservatives—so called because many of them were former Democrats who had converted to Republicanism—along with other like thinkers who could not strictly be called neo-conservatives, viewed Israel as a vital strategic bastion against Soviet advances in the Middle East and regarded the Palestinians as tools of the Soviet Union. Reagan himself thought of the Palestinian problem as "one of history's running sores" that should just be left to Israel to resolve, and these neo-conservatives and their friends took the same position: anything that strengthened Israel in the fight against the Soviets was all to the good, whether this was arms and economic aid from the United States or Israel's steady consolidation of control over and settlement expansion in the Occupied Territories. The neo-conservatives in the Reagan era were not just anti-Soviet; they were fiercely pro-Israeli and actively hostile to any notion of Palestinian nationalism.

There is every reason to believe that they remain as pro-Israeli and anti-Palestinian today, even though the Soviet fulcrum has disappeared. Are they influencing policy? It is difficult to say precisely how much, but the answer is clearly "yes." It is well known that they are lobbying heavily, and have been since the early days of the Bush administration—well before 11 September—for some kind of action against Iraq. They have not won their point yet, but they have turned up the volume since 11 September, and they are certainly having an impact on policy planning. As I think we all know, Deputy Secretary of Defense Paul Wolfowitz has talked about "ending states" that support terrorism, and a group of neo-conservatives and others, affectionately known in the press as the "Wolfowitz cabal," is trying to build a case against Iraq.

This group has also had an apparent influence on how the administration has framed its war against terrorism. This is an interesting example, in fact, of how influence is used within policymaking circles and how a mindset can be shaped. In the first week or so after the incidents of 11 September, the Bush team was grappling with how best to focus the nation's attention and energy on the struggle ahead—a way that would seem to give the struggle a moral grounding, that would not insult Muslims or appear to be raising a crusade against Islam, and that would avoid turning any attention on U.S. policies, particularly on grievances arising out of U.S. policies as possible "root causes" of terrorism. So the neo-conservatives turned to one of their own—a law professor named David Forte who had served as Jeane Kirkpatrick's legal counsel when she was ambassador to the UN.

Forte had written some articles on Osama bin Laden, maintaining essentially that he and his radical associates are criminals and fascists whose only agenda is spreading their ultra-conservative brand of Islam and defeating anyone who opposes them. The day after the terrorism in New York and Washington, another former Reagan administration official circulated Forte's writings among the network of neo-conservatives now in the administration. The article went to John Bolton, Douglas Feith, and Elliot Abrams, and—presto!—some of Forte's phraseology made its way into President Bush's address to Congress a week later.

The message in the Forte writings was twofold: first, that bin Laden and his radicals do not represent Islam, but have actually corrupted Islam's teachings to further their own heinous objectives. That much is correct enough, but exclusive reliance on this argument leads to another conclusion that is very wrong and very dangerous. This feeds the notion that bin Laden and his associates oppose us because of what we are, not because of what we do, and the natural conclusion is therefore that he is nothing but an unregenerate fanatic and the United States need do nothing except pursue its war—that it need not examine its own policies to determine if there is anything about them that breeds the kind of hatred that might provoke terrorism. The conclusion, in other words, is that there are no root causes for the terrorism—no legitimate grievances against Israel for its treatment of the Palestinians, no legitimate grievances against the United States for its support for Israel's actions, or for its sanctions against Iraq, or for its assertion of economic and political and military hegemony throughout the Muslim world. If you can write off bin Laden and *al-Qaeda* as causeless fanatics, you are relieved of any obligation to address causes, and Israel is let off the hook.

This is obviously the conclusion drawn by the neo-conservatives in and around the administration, as well as most U.S. supporters of Israel and Israel itself: that the United States bears no responsibility whatsoever in all this, that Israel has no responsibility, and that no policy changes are necessary. I think the jury is still out on whether the administration has entirely taken this argument aboard, but at the moment, it certainly seems to have.

This brings me to the question of continuity and difference between administrations. It is actually a mixed picture with regard to Palestinian-Israeli issues. There clearly are differences among all administrations—differences particularly in the casts of characters and the impact these characters have on policy formulation and implementation. The influence of the neo-conservatives in the Reagan administration, together with Reagan's own and Secretary of State Shultz's anti-Palestinian sentiments, made that a very different administration with different policy inclinations from the Bush Senior administration that immediately followed it.

Bush himself was a consummate pragmatist with no emotional investment in any foreign policy issue or any country. His secretary of state, James Baker, was even more unsentimental. Neither one had any particular feeling for Israel, and both intensely disliked Yitzhak Shamir, who was Israel's prime minister during the first three years of that administration. This did not make Bush and Baker friends of the Palestinians, but it did incline them toward a greater willingness to confront Shamir's intransigence about starting peace negotiations and toward clearly asserting the U.S. right to make demands of Israel in spite of Shamir's opposition. This willingness to stand up to Israel, which was essentially a function of their personalities, made the Bush-Baker policy orientation very different from that of the neo-conservatives who had preceded them, quite different also from later Clinton administration policymaking, and different even from the policy inclinations of the George W. Bush administration. As I suggested earlier, the lineage of this apple is only partially traceable to his father's tree.

All that said, I think it remains true that continuity, rather than difference, is the dominant reality. Differences of personality can and do produce differences in policy, but they are usually only in degree and they are usually fleeting, lasting only as long as the unique personalities are in office. In fact, I think the Bush-Baker attitude toward Israel and their willingness to oppose Israel actively on the settlements issue must be considered merely an aberration in the long continuous history of U.S. accommodation of Israel. The fundamental reality is that, with the possible exception of Jimmy Carter's, all administrations—even going back as far as World War I—have approached the conflict over Palestine from a perspective oriented toward Israel and almost totally oblivious to Palestinian concerns.

The late scholar Malcolm Kerr wrote in 1980 that the conventional wisdom about the origins of the Arab-Israeli conflict had become so entrenched throughout the United States that serious discourse had ceased among the public and, except in rare instances, even among policymakers, and diplomats were severely inhibited in their ability to formulate innovative policy. Policymakers, he thought, were so much inclined to avoid controversy that it had long since become the tendency among the very people inside government whose job it was to study the issues, to fall back instead on the analysis prevailing in Congress, in the press, and among the general public. I believe his analysis remains as true today, despite great changes in the conflict, as it was two decades ago.

Perceptions rather than realities on the ground have always played the dominant role in shaping public attitudes and policymaker thinking on the Palestinian-Israeli conflict, and the general perception, from one administration to the next, has always been of Israelis as victims, peace-loving but uncompromising in their determination to survive, and of Palestinians as hate-filled, animated by no legitimate grievances and, underneath everything, determined to exterminate Israel. Policymakers are ultimately ordinary people like the rest of us, who absorb the ideas and beliefs that dominate society as they come of age, and it is important to note that since the early twentieth century, no generation of American policymakers has ever grown up without internalizing an extremely negative image of all Arabs, and an extremely favorable image of Israelis, from the perceptions prevalent throughout society.

This makes a huge difference in how policymakers—I am talking here about presidents and secretaries of state and their political advisers, rather than about middle-level policymakers at the State Department or on the National Security Council staff—approach the problem when they begin to mediate the conflict, or when they try to negotiate a cease-fire, or when they just examine what the issues are. It takes a lot of knowledge and a lot of study to understand the nuances of the issues involved and particularly to overcome the misperceptions and distortions in commonly held viewpoints.

Just to give an example, a month ago the *Economist* ran a long article on the history of U.S. involvement with Israel and the peace process that was so filled with myth and distortion that it read like a Likud Party propaganda tract. A friend asked me to comment on it, which I did by inserting comments in brackets into the text on a computer file. Not only did the effort take me hours, but I actually doubled the length of the piece by trying to clarify it. A Palestinian-American woman once told me in frustration that it takes "books and books of history just to explain why falafel is not Israeli," and then when she goes into that history, people back off from her in horror—she is an agitator or even a terrorist. Edward Said has written the same thing more elegantly: "I feel impelled," he says, "to bring logic, history, and rhetoric to my aid, at tedious length. We need to retell our story from scratch every time." These statements were made in the 1980s, but nothing has really changed since then—as has been amply demonstrated by the last year-plus of gross misunderstanding and deliberate myth-making over what happened at the Camp David summit and why the *intifada* erupted.

I do not think most presidents and secretaries of state have ever had even a superficial knowledge of those books and books of history—or indeed any of the knowledge necessary to understand *both* sides of the conflict they are mediating. Nor have they taken the time to gain the knowledge. Going back just 20 years: Ronald Reagan and George Shultz and their neo-conservatives certainly had no understanding whatsoever of the Palestinian perspective, and they actively shunned any effort to learn. George Bush the elder and James Baker did gain a good insight into the Israeli settlements, the motivation behind them, and the great obstacle they pose to working toward peace on the ground, but even this was only one aspect of the problem.

Bill Clinton prided himself on being able to draw a map of the West Bank in his sleep, and maybe he could, but he and his very Israeli-oriented advisers had no knowledge of what Israel's continued occupation, continued settlement, continued colonization meant to the daily lives and the national prospects of the Palestinians. At the time of the Camp David summit last year, sources around Clinton were even talking to the press about the difficulty they had relating to the Palestinians. And I have to say that George W. Bush seems to have taken in very little from his father's experience with the conflict. His knowledge of Israel and Palestine seems to have come at least initially from a helicopter ride with Ariel Sharon some years ago, and I would question whether he has any appreciation for the sad irony and the inequity in the situation demonstrated by the fact that the Palestinians not only do not own a helicopter in which to show visiting dignitaries how small their territory is, but would not be allowed to fly in the airspace over their land even if they had one.

Obviously, President Bush has learned more and gained more perspective since that helicopter ride—he is now talking about the need for a Palestinian state—but it is important to understand that now, perhaps more than at any time in the past, the political culture in the United States makes it almost impossible to gain a balanced view of the conflict. The distractions of 11 September and its aftermath militate against any serious reassessment of where the Palestinian-Israeli issue stands; the domestic political risks of confronting Israel are almost overwhelming; public receptivity to the Palestinian point of view is virtually nil at the moment and sympathy for Israel is high; there are those neo-conservatives nattering and pressuring on the right; and the media—which create the atmosphere in which we all, policymakers included, form our most basic impressions—have shown more vicious anti-Palestinian bias than at any time since the 1970s.

Particularly before taking office, Bush and his advisers must inevitably have absorbed the same venomous rhetoric that the rest of us read and hear *ad nauseam*—about the "breathtakingly generous" Israeli offer at Camp David that Arafat rejected without so much as a counterproposal, about the Palestinians' deep-seated desire to exterminate Israel as demonstrated by their resort to violence in the *intifada,* about the threat to Israel's existence posed by the terrorist Arafat, about the Palestinians' inability to give Israel unequivocal acceptance. This is the way Middle East policy is often made in Washington in fact—through the commentary of leading opinion-molders like Thomas Friedman and others who spout these distortions all the time and whose critical position at the center of public discourse enables them to influence public thinking and at the same time reflect that thinking upward to policymakers.

The long and the short of the situation—of the so-called perceptions of Palestine—is that there has never been room in American political discourse, at any level, for the Palestinian perspective. Despite years of U.S. peacemaking, it is still the case that, in the minds of most Americans, policymakers included, the Palestinians' stake in the peace process, and their stake in Palestine, is in no way equal to Israel's. Perhaps even more serious, the level of understanding of what Palestinian objectives are remains abysmal. The image of Palestinians as motivated solely by hatred of Jews rather than by real grievances is not new, but after years in which the Palestinians had begun to be accepted by public opinion as legitimate participants in the peace process, the extent and intensity of today's poisonous atmosphere are startling.

What is most disturbing is that policymakers have bought into this mood. Bill Clinton and Dennis Ross still regale the lecture circuit and the Manhattan cocktail party circuit with tales of how the Palestinians just wallow in their grievances and their hatred and are incapable of making a "strategic decision for peace." Despite his recent "vision" of a Palestinian state, George W. Bush still treats Arafat like a terrorist, denying him, and therefore the Palestinian people, any legitimacy, allowing Israel to define the Palestinians, and accepting all of Israel's actions—including its settlement expansion and land confiscation, its assassination of Palestinians, its killing of Palestinian children, its reoccupation of West Bank cities—with, at most, apologetic verbal complaints but no concrete objection. This is not the action of an administration interested in honestly brokering an equitable peace agreement.

The principal mantra of both the Clinton and the George W. Bush administrations has been that the United States "cannot want peace more than the parties do," and that therefore there is little we can do to move things along toward peace or away from warfare until the parties are ready. But this kind of hands-off approach and this studied neutrality is false neutrality. In actuality, this is fundamentally an Israel-centered policy, not a neutral policy.

You cannot *be* neutral, as Clinton and Bush have tried to be by not taking a position on the key issues, if you are underwriting the vastly stronger side in a conflict with massive aid. When one side controls all the land under negotiation and has all the military power, any policy put forth by a mediator to support the *status quo* and just wait for the parties to reach agreement on their own automatically predetermines the outcome of the negotiations in favor of the stronger side. In the same way, the Bush administration is encouraging continued violence by not taking any steps to end it. Because of its massive aid to Israel, the United States is an enabler rather than a helpful mediator. By continuing to arm only one side in the conflict and thereby enabling Israel to resist making concessions, while at the same time refusing to address the Palestinian grievances that are at the root of the uprising, the United States is simply perpetuating the fighting and violence. Just as you cannot, as a mediator, simply sit back and wait for the parties to reach a negotiated agreement on their own when the two sides are so unbalanced, you also cannot, as a mediator, just sit back and wait for them to cease firing when you are the one arming the stronger side. It is the height of cynicism to plead powerlessness in this situation.

Guaranteeing Israel's existence has been a pillar of U.S. Middle East policy since 1948, and ensuring Israel's security has been the U.S. objective throughout the peace process. This is appropriate, but the problem with U.S. peacemaking—and the basic reason the peace process collapsed—has been that no one considers the need to give equal guarantees of Palestinian security and Palestinian existence as a nation. The United States must begin to look at the conflict from the perspective of both sides: it must ask itself whether Israel would live in the kind of truncated, non-viable, indefensible state that we have been trying to foist on the Palestinians; it must become as concerned to guarantee Palestinian security and preserve the Palestinians' national existence as it is to guarantee Israel's security and existence. Until that time, the United States will never be able to bring peace to Palestinians and Israelis; nor will it have much chance of winning its war on terrorism.

Kathleen Christison was a political analyst with the CIA for 16 years, dealing with the Middle East for eight years. She is a freelance writer, dealing with the Palestinian-Israeli conflict and has published articles and book reviews in several Middle East journals.

American Media Coverage
Of the Current *Intifada*

by Edward S. Herman

In her book *Beyond Belief,* Deborah Lipstadt showed that during the years of the Holocaust, Jews were treated as unworthy victims by the mainstream American media. Reports of mass murder were placed on the back pages, sometimes near the comic strips, even in papers like the *New York Times* and the *Washington Post,* owned by Jewish proprietors. At that time, anti-Semitism was strong, the Jewish establishment was fearful and weak, and the condition of European Jews was of little concern to the U.S. political leadership.

This situation changed slowly but steadily after the end of World War II, as anti-Semitism weakened, the Jewish establishment became stronger and more aggressively supportive of Israel, and Israel became a cog in U.S. foreign policy, receiving massive aid and military support. American mainstream media treatment of the Jews and Israel reversed itself accordingly—the Jews in Israel became worthy, and *their* victims became unworthy. This reversal was institutionalized many decades back, and has never flagged as the American mainstream media have followed closely their government's agenda of giving Israel virtual carte blanche in dealing with their Palestinian subjects—both within Israel and in the Occupied Territories. This has applied through both *intifadas,* and the resultant overwhelming media bias remains obvious today.

This bias is evident from structural facts, such as the massive presence of mainstream media owners, editors, commentators, and pundits who are openly—and sometimes passionately—pro-Israel. These include Mortimer Zuckerman, George Will, Fred Barnes, William Safire, A. M. Rosenthal, Robert Bartley, Martin Peretz, Charles Krauthammer, Cal Thomas, Morton Kondracke, William Kristol, and many others, with Derrick Z. Jackson of the *Boston Globe* virtually alone as a regular columnist supporting the Palestinians, and lacking national outreach. Apart from Jackson, the "left" on this issue in the media calls for reasonableness and restraint on both sides, but does not accuse Israel of systematic ethnic cleansing or call for forcing the Israelis to exit the Occupied Territories. A noted examplar, Anthony Lewis, even celebrated an Israeli court decision calling for the end to torture with an op-ed entitled "A Light unto the Nations."

The bias on the Israeli-Palestinian conflict is sometimes illustrated dramatically in events. For instance, long-time *New York Times* Executive Editor A. M. Rosenthal received an award in 1991 as "Defender of Jerusalem" for his "passionate voice on Jewish and Israeli affairs" (Rosenthal refused to allow an unpleasant fact about Rabbi Meier Kahane to be published because it "would generate anti-Semitism"), and CBS news anchor Dan Rather enthusiastically participated, contrary to CBS rules, in a 1992 Jerusalem Foundation fund-raiser chaired by pro-Israel hawks Martin Peretz and Mortimer Zuckerman. But the bias is on continual display in actual media performance.

We can see this in the language used by the media, the frames they apply, and what they feature and suppress. These have long contributed to the normalization of a system of discrimination, expropriation, and terror by the dominant party—Israel—that keeps the abuse of the unworthy victims out of public consciousness and allows it to continue unimpeded.

Language: Ethnic cleansing, violence, terrorism, clashes

Consider language. In media reporting on the second *intifada,* "violence" means stone-throwing and shooting. It never refers to "structural violence" such as expropriating land, evicting people from their houses and demolishing them, seizing and diverting water resources for the use of the Israelis, building roads that destroy communities' access to former neighbors and jobs, directly closing down access by army orders and barricades, and tolerating and protecting settlers' attacks, including the destruction and seizure of Gentile property. Even though there have been a substantial number of killings and injuries inflicted on the Gentiles by the army and settlers in this process, this massive low-intensity violence has been entirely acceptable to the Clinton, George W. Bush, and preceding administrations. So for the mainstream media it is not classified as violence or given serious attention.

Similarly, the media have continued their long tradition of finding the Palestinians terrorists, the Israelis victims—even "under siege"—and engaging only in retaliation. Almost without exception, the media make deadly Palestinian actions terrorism, and attach indignant language. The killing of two Israeli soldiers was a "sickening lynch-murder," a Palestinian attack on a settlers' bus was "unspeakable" and a "terrorist outrage" in the *New York Times,* but none of the more than 600 Palestinian deaths have been worthy of such adjectives. Thus, regarding a massive Israeli bombardment of a civilian area in Gaza, this was "predictably … a strong Israeli response" to a previous bombing of a settlers' bus. Only the Israelis respond and retaliate, and do this "predictably," meaning responsively and reasonably. "Yesterday's Palestinian terrorism and Israeli retaliation … " (editorial, *New York Times,* 21 November 2000) is the formulaic language of deep bias. Norman Solomon reports that a Nexis search of American media for the first 100 days of 2001 found several dozen references to Israeli "retaliation," but only one instance where Palestinian actions were deemed retaliatory.

When the Palestinians kill an Israeli leader, this is terrorism. When the Israelis kill Palestinian leaders, it is not terrorism, but "assassination" of terrorists. On the day after the 11 September World Trade Center and Pentagon bombings, Clyde Haberman wrote in the *New York Times,* "Do you get it now?" suggesting that the American public could now understand why Israel used force against the Palestinians. It would not occur to Haberman, or his colleagues, that this might help understand Palestinian violence against Israelis.

By the same bias, Israeli Prime Minister Ariel Sharon, whose responsibility for killing unarmed civilians exceeds that of Carlos the Jackal by a factor of 20 or more, is never a "terrorist" or "war criminal" in the mainstream media, although occasionally it is said that "they," meaning Arabs, so designate him. Instead, he has a "new air of electability" (*Philadelphia Inquirer,* 7 January 2001), is "tough" and a "warrior" (*New York Times* front page, 7 February 2001), or an "old soldier"

(*New York Times,* 7 February 2001). Shortly after the Sabra and Shatila massacre, he was described as "the forceful general intent on security for Israel" (*New York Times,* 11 February 1983).

For U.S. officials, the "security" issue in the Israeli-Palestinian conflict refers to Israeli security, and this is reflected in media usage. I have never seen a mainstream media article that has discussed the problem of "Palestinian security," although the death and injury ratio over many years, and the inequality in armaments, suggests that the Palestinians are more needful of security than the Israelis. This linguistic double standard reflects deep bias.

Robert Fisk says that when he reads of death in "a cross-fire" or "clashes" he knows that this means the Israelis did the killing. Fisk also notes how easily the media refer to a "suspected Palestinian gunman" or "presumably by Palestinians" when Israelis are shot at, whereas Palestinians always die "in clashes … as if they were accidentally shot rather than targets for Israeli snipers."

Bias in critical frames

Framing bias is closely linked to bias in language, and the American mainstream media uses words like terrorism and violence to describe the retail acts of the Palestinians, but not the wholesale killings and coerced structural changes imposed by the Israelis. They also refuse to use the words "ethnic cleansing" to describe Israeli policy, despite the excellence of the fit. But there *are* powerful frames that do put the locus of blame for violence on the ethnic cleansing state and its sponsor. These critical frames, spelled out by Israeli journalists like Amira Hass and Danny Rubenstein, are as scarce as hens' teeth in the American mainstream press, although they flourish in the alternative media.

The primary alternative frame we may call the injustice model. Amira Hass writing in *Ha'aretz* employs such a critical frame in explaining the second *intifada* as an inevitable response to the complete failure of Oslo to do anything whatever for the Palestinians, and their further decline in welfare and morale. Robert Fisk says the same: that the *intifada* "is what happens when a whole society is pressure-cooked to the point of explosion." Hass, Fisk, Rubenstein, and other reporters and analysts have given similar interpretations stressing continued expropriations by settlers and the army, the hugely racist and humiliating treatment meted out to the Palestinians by their overlords, and the fact that recent Israeli-U.S. plans not only ratify the illegal, post-Oslo "facts on the ground," but provide for no meaningful resolution of the refugee crisis, no credible East Jerusalem sovereignty, and no viable and independent Palestinian state.

In this critical frame, the Palestinian uprising is rooted in extreme abuse and injustice, disappointed hopes, disillusionment with both Oslo and the Arafat leadership, and the final provocation of Sharon and Barak at al-Aqsa. The explosion was widely expected, "predictable," and understandable, and in these senses it was a "rational" response to extreme abuse and the absence of peaceable options.

Almost without exception the American mainstream media frame their presentations of the issues in the Israeli-Palestinian conflict so as to apologize for Israeli policy and put the blame for any violence on Israel's victims.

The "Palestinian irrationality and stubbornness" model utilizes phrases such as "Barak's generous offer," "Arafat's war," and "irrational Palestinian outburst." Essential ingredients of this dominant mainstream frame are the assumptions that Barak was a "moderate" and that his offers and the "peace process" have been reasonable, so that any disturbances or uprisings are therefore irresponsible, unjustifiable, or irrational. Absolutely essential to propagating this frame is the refusal to discuss issues of justice or to evaluate them in detail. You will never find Thomas Friedman discussing the Israeli policy of systematic expropriation of Palestinians in the Occupied Territories, the demolitions, the appropriation of water for Jewish use, the doubled settler population since 1993, the road construction that makes a Palestinian state unviable, or the policy of killing and injuring Gentiles freely, but not Jews.

In "Arafat's War" *(New York Times,* 13 October 2000), which gives us Friedman's standard model—characteristic of the *Times* as an institution, and predominant throughout the mainstream media—Friedman mentions the "old complaints about the brutality of the continued Israeli occupation and settlement building. Frankly, the Israeli checkpoints and continued settlement building are oppressive." He finesses this huge set of issues by making them "old" (stale), and avoiding details, numbers, or discussion of the racist violence in expropriation for Israeli Jews only, the large-scale violations of the Fourth Geneva Convention, or the beggaring of the Palestinians under Oslo. He also argues that such matters are now irrelevant because Barak has offered "unprecedented compromises," so that if the Palestinians do not fall in line with these, any violence is their fault.

"Arafat's War" rests on the failure of the Palestinians to acknowledge total defeat: their unwillingness to accept all the past injustices, including post-1993 expropriations, a *bantustan* system worse than that imposed by South Africa under apartheid, and continued military domination by a country that has been a wee bit "oppressive" (Clinton and Barak demanded a demilitarized Palestinian state, and continued Israeli occupation rights in the West Bank, out of consideration for Israeli security). If Arafat would not accept this, and sign another imprecise agreement that once again left much to the goodwill of Israel and its sponsor, all the violence is his doing.

This "Palestinian irrationality and stubbornness model" amounts to crude apologetics for ethnic cleansing. And it was hardly confined to Friedman and the *New York Times* editorial pages. It was pretty standard in the news, as well as editorial pages, that it was Arafat's choice of "Peace or Victimhood" (Jane Perlez, "Fork in Arafat's Road," *New York Times,* 29 December 2000). Israel is not required to make a choice because the *status quo* that it supports is taken as a given.

Other establishment frames feature Arafat and the return to terrorism, with regular media references to Arafat's responsibility for failing to contain the violence, speculations on whether he actually stirred it up to improve his bargaining position with Israel, and admonitions to Arafat to get his people under control. In another frame, the mainstream media have latched onto the claim that the Palestinians are callously pushing their children forward to die, that they suffer from a martyr syndrome, and that the parents, Arafat, and the penchant toward martyrdom are therefore responsible for the numerous shooting deaths of children (Chris Hedges, "The Deathly Glamour of Martydom," *New York Times,* 29 October 2000).

Two other frames are also worthy of note. One is that the United States is an honest broker, and that it, not the UN or other less involved countries, should be the one to bring peace and justice to the Israeli-Palestinian conflict. As this country has used its veto some 60 times on behalf of Israel, reassures it continuously of its solidarity, and also backs Israel with some $3 billion in annual aid, and Israel's long-term "redemption of the land" under U.S. auspices—and incessant conflict—are guaranteed, the honest broker role is a sick joke. That the media accept it displays their deep bias.

So does their "patience" model. The media refer regularly to Israeli patience being tried. With reference to the Serbs, by contrast, the Serb failure to contain their state's violence against the Kosovo Albanians was not "patience," it was guilty support, with the Serbs, "guilty executioners." The contrast displays deep bias.

Emphases, suppression of inconvenient facts, and normalization

It is possible to report inconvenient facts, but so sparsely, so devoid of human-interest detail, that they can be overlooked and normalized. This was long and dramatically illustrated by the media treatment of the Israeli torture of Palestinians. When the *London Times* did an extensive study of Israeli torture back in 1977, the *New York Times* and the *Washington Post* both declined the opportunity to use the original materials. The *New York Times'* first installment in the report, on a back page, featured Israeli denials and included none of the substantive findings of the *London Times* study. In 1993 and 1994, when Israeli torture of Palestinians was running at 400-500 victims per month, a rare *New York Times* article on the subject mentioned the numbers being tortured quite matter-of-factly, deep within an article that stressed Israeli doubts about the merits of the ongoing "interrogation practices" (Joel Greenberg, "Israel Rethinking Interrogation of Arabs," *New York Times,* 14 August 1993). Had they been Serb "interrogation practices" in Kosovo, they would have been featured intensively and with great indignation. Treated as they were in Israel, they normalized this terrible practice.

Visual aversion has been extremely important in protecting the approved system of institutionalized injustice and ethnic cleansing. Thus, the American mainstream media simply will not discuss the laws applying to an occupying power and their responsibilities under the Fourth Geneva Convention, and Israel's massive violations of these rules in expropriations, discriminatory use of water, and other matters are barely noted. The violence of Israel in imprisonment, torture, beatings, killings, and injuries, as well as aid and protection to settler violence, is enormously greater than Palestinian violence against Israel, but it is downplayed and relevant information on these matters is subjected to massive suppression.

During the current *intifada* the media have reported on Israeli attacks and "assassinations," but they have given greater attention and exclusive indignation to stone throwing and suicide bombings by Palestinians than to the more cruel and deadly violence of the Israeli army. The better than four-to-one ratio of killings, and far higher ratio of Palestinian injuries to those of Israelis, is neutralized by greater attention to, and much greater humanization of, Israeli victims. In a simple and rough measure of this bias, of eight front page photos of *intifada* victims in the *New York Times* from 28 September 2000 through 9 March 2001, six were of Israelis and two were of Palestinians. This helps sustain the identification of "violence" with the stone throwing and suicide bombing of the population in revolt.

The past month's large-scale Israeli invasion and occupation of Palestinian-controlled cities in the Occupied Territories has been given relatively low-key treatment by the media, featuring Israeli explanations, admonitions from the Bush administration, admissions that such attacks were made easier by the new post-11 September "anti-terrorist" campaign, and brief Palestinian outcries. In reports on the Israeli campaign there was no mention that in its midst the Senate approved a $2.8 billion aid bill for Israel, or the fact that Israel violates the arms export act daily in targeting population centers in an offensive war. Most important, the scale of destruction, the damage to medical facilities, schools, water and sanitary equipment, and homes, and the climate of fear this has engendered, have been essentially suppressed. As in the past, devastating and humanizing reports by the Physicians for Human Rights-Israel, B'Tselem, and Amnesty International were not cited, nor was Bethlehem University's touching "Appeal for Protection" of 24 October ever mentioned. The media prefer to cite Sharon, Colin Powell, other Israeli and American officials, and an occasional Palestinian. In the process, serious state terrorism is normalized, as in a long tradition.

Conclusion

Robert Fisk notes that "Oddly, you can now learn more from the Israeli press than the American media. The brutality of Israeli soldiers is fully covered in *Ha'aretz*, which also reports on the large number of American negotiators who are Jewish. Four years ago, a former Israeli soldier described in an Israeli newspaper how his men had looted a village in southern Lebanon. When the piece was reprinted in the *New York Times,* the looting episode was censored out of the text" (*Independent,* 13 December 2000).

The American mainstream media's coverage of Middle East issues shows a genuine propaganda system in action. They have done a truly outstanding job of supporting state policy by making Israel's ethnic cleansing palatable, finding the victims the source of the violence, and thus facilitating virtually any level of wholesale violence Israel deems necessary to protect itself against "terrorism." As its ethnic cleansing policies inevitably produce secondary reactions to the primary (Israeli) violence, the media contribute to an escalating process with no decent end in sight.

Edward Herman, Professor Emeritus of Finance at the Wharton School of the University of Pennsylvania, has been a contributor to Z Magazine *since its founding in 1988. He is the author of numerous books, including a number of corporate and media studies.*

Appendix 1: Suppressed evidence

Let me give a small sample illustrative of suppressions, taken from a very large pool, by type. It should be noted that what is suppressed are very often reports by UN bodies, human rights groups, Palestinian and Arab sources, and other individuals and reporters who fail to meet agenda standards. They put Israel in too bad a light, or mention U.S. military or counterinsurgency aid not helpful to the image of an honest broker. Barak, Sharon, Israeli army sources, and U.S. officials, although hugely biased and guilty of repeated lies, are the steady basis of the "news" agenda, which explains why whether Arafat can control the violence is an issue, but not whether Barak, Sharon, Clinton, or Bush can do the same.

UN documents:

1.	"UN Special Report on Israel for the Committee on Economic, Social, and Cultural Rights," dated 13 November 2000, strongly condemning Israeli violations of the Geneva Convention, Oslo agreement, and human rights, was not mentioned in the American media.

2.	UN report of 26 February 2001, which described the Israeli closures on the West Bank and Gaza as being "the most severe and sustained set of movement restrictions imposed on the Occupied Palestinian Territory since the beginning of the occupation in 1967," was completely ignored in the American mainstream media.

Amnesty International and Human Rights Watch reports:

1.	Human Rights Watch's (HRW) report, charging that "Israeli soldiers have abused hundreds of Palestinian drivers, beating them and slashing their car tires on roads in the West Bank," released on 27 February was not cited anywhere in the American mainstream media.

2.	HRW's report of 11 April 2001, "Center of the Storm," was called "a very severe report on the killing and wounding of Palestinian civilians in Hebron by Israeli Defense Forces soldiers and Jewish settlers." It was featured twice in *Ha'aretz* and once in London's *Independent,* but was only mentioned in passing in the *Washington Post* (16 April 2001), and was otherwise entirely blacked out in the American media.

3. Amnesty International's (AI) report of 8 December 1999 on the Israeli policy of house demolitions was unreported in the American mainstream media.

4. AI's report of 26 October 2000 charging that Israel's failure to investigate deaths cheapens life was mentioned briefly in the *Washington Post* (2 November) and *Boston Globe* (2 November), but was featured nowhere in the mainstream media.

5. AI's 3 November 2000 report condemning Israel's attacks on civilians was mentioned in the *Los Angeles Times* (5 November), but was not featured there or mentioned elsewhere.

6. AI's 9 November 2000 report charging that mass arrests in Jerusalem and northern Israel are often followed by police beatings was mentioned (but not featured) only in the *Chicago Tribune* (15 November), *Chicago Sun-Times* (14 November), and *The Oregonian* (16 November).

7. AI's 24 November 2000 call for the deployment of human rights observers was mentioned only in the *New York Times* on the back page and dismissively (28 November 2000), and in *The Deseret News* (25 November 2000).

8. AI's 24 January 2001 report charging impunity in the case of the killing of Palestinians (specifically criticizing a nominal sentence for a settler's murder of an eleven-year-old Palestinian child) was unmentioned in the mainstream media.

**Evidence of American supply of deadly weapons
and counterinsurgency support and training:**

1. The Hebrew weekly *Kol Ha'ir* reported on 26 January 2001 that "U.S. Marines Trained with Tsahal [IDF] for Reconquest of the Territories of the Palestinian Authority." Picked up by *Agence France Presse* on 27 January 2001, this was unreported in the American media.

2. Defense journals and Boeing reported the Boeing sale of nine Apache Longbow helicopters to Israel in February 2001, but the mainstream media failed to report this transaction (and other major weapons sales and transfers to Israel were of equal disinterest).

3. Israel and the "honest broker" also carried out joint exercises in February 2001 to test Patriot air defense missiles transferred from U.S. bases in Germany to Israel. This evidence of an extremely close military relationship

between the two countries was mentioned in passing in the *Washington Post* (20 February 2001), but nowhere else in the mainstream media.

Evidence of exceptional Israeli cruelty:

1. The Palestine Monitor reported on 19 March 2001, that "Israeli soldiers at Al Ram checkpoint fired tear gas canisters and sound bombs directly at Palestinians participating in a peaceful women's march. Soldiers beat the women with the butts of their rifles. Fifteen women were transported to nearby hospitals. The march was organized by the Union of Palestinian Women's Committees to protest the continued Israeli imposed closure and siege on the Occupied Palestinian Territories. Eyewitnesses reported that the march from Ramallah to the Al Ram checkpoint was completely peaceful from the Palestinian side." This incident was unreported in the American media.

2. On 20 February 2001, the National School for Blind Girls in al-Bireh was shelled by Israeli tanks and heavy weaponry for three hours, seriously damaging the building and terrifying the disabled girls. The attacks apparently resulted because unknown parties had fired upon a nearby Jewish settlement. This incident was unreported in the American mainstream media.

3. In early January 2001 a ten-year-old Palestinian girl Ella Ahmed in El Sawiya, near Nablus, died of a burst appendix after Israeli soldiers twice refused to allow passage to a hospital in Nablus. This was reported in *Ha'aretz* on 9 January, but was not picked up in the American media.

4. Sabreen Balout was born in a taxi on 24 January 2001, as the Israeli Defense Forces refused to allow passage to a hospital. They insisted that the passengers in the taxi, including the baby still linked to her mother by an umbilical cord, get out of the cab on a cold rainy night. This was reported in *Ha'aretz*, but not in the American media.

5. United Nations Relief and Works Agency (UNRWA) Director Peter Hansen issued an unusual press release and report on 11 March 2001. It declared that Israeli policy in the West Bank and Gaza in destroying roads, uprooting trees, and damaging agricultural land in the interest of "security," not only violated international norms and laws, it threatened a "humanitarian catastrophe." This UNRWA material was not picked up in the American mainstream media.

Appendix 2: Normalizing structural violence: Demolitions

The media's treatment of Israel's systematic demolitions of Palestinian homes provides an enlightening case study in bias. The policy of demolitions is horrendously inhumane and, with its racist concentration on Palestinian homes, is reminiscent of Nazi practice. There has been a steady stream of stories on the internet— issued by the Ethnic NewsWatch, Israeli Committee Against House Demolitions (ICHAD), the Palestinian Land Defense Committee (PLDC), Christian Peacemaker Teams (CPT), the Hebron Solidarity Committee (HSC), and other groups— describing army demolitions that push Palestinians out virtually without notice.

These stories are numerous, dramatic, and often heartbreaking, as Jewish Israeli protesters and Christian teams often struggle to protect Palestinians from the racist onslaught of the army and the settlers. The stories often describe demolitions of houses being rebuilt by protesters and then being bulldozed out of existence by the army for a second or third time. AI issued a report on this savage policy. That report stressed the policy's racist basis, widespread Palestinian fear of demolitions, and the murderous character of the policy. In one case, 100 border police came without notice and started to destroy a house. Palestinians started to throw stones, and the police killed Zaki 'Ubayd, a 28-year-old father. The free press ignored this report.

A Nexis search of coverage of demolitions of Palestinian homes in the *New York Times,* the *Washington Post,* the *Los Angeles Times, Time,* and *Newsweek* for the five years from 1 January 1996 through 31 December 2000, comes up with only 23 articles: none in *Time,* one in *Newsweek,* five in the *New York Times,* eleven in the *Washington Post,* and six in the *Los Angeles Times.* With only a single exception in the *Washington Post,* these articles never mention the Israeli Committee Against Demolitions, the Hebron Solidarity Committee, and the Palestinian Land Defense Committee. Only two of the 23 articles made the front page, and only five give substantial detail on the brutality of the practice, and the suffering of the Palestinian victims. Twenty of the twenty-three give the Israeli rationale that the Palestinian homes were illegally built, and nine describe the demolitions as a response to Palestinian violence. Only six note that Palestinians are not allowed to build, and only one suggests even indirectly that the demolitions and settlements violate the Oslo accords as well as the Fourth Geneva Convention.

In that single exceptional case, Steven Erlanger says "[w]hile Labor governments have also expanded existing settlements and the Oslo accords do not limit them from doing so, the Palestinians have complained that Israel now builds large new neighborhoods near existing settlements in order to call them expansion, rather than label them new" *(New York Times,* 12 September 1997). Note first that Erlanger's statement that Oslo does not preclude expanding settlements is strictly the Israeli interpretation of general language, and he cannot admit that new settlements have taken place, but only speaks of Palestinian complaints. He does not discuss whether doubling the number of settlers and other Israeli actions might possibly violate the spirit of Oslo.

In sum, in a period of intense demolition activity by Israel, the five print media examined treated the issue in a very low-key way, with zero editorial attention. They created a false sense of balance by giving serious weight to alleged building code violations and responses to Palestinian terrorism as the basis for Israeli policy. They downplayed the violations of Oslo and international law, the hugely discriminatory features of Israeli law, and the direct terrorist abuses of the army and settlers in demolishing and taking over Palestinian property. They handled the issue in such a manner that the American public would hardly know of this practice, and would hardly be roused to indignation, in contrast with their responses to the media's focus on Palestinian stone throwing and other misbehavior.

Humanitarian Law
And U.S. Foreign Policy

by Richard Falk

This conference comes at an important time because the events of 11 September create both an opportunity and a danger associated with the Palestinian-Israeli conflict that requires a rethinking of how one might view the future and of the best response at the present time. Humanitarian law and international law are still relevant to an understanding of the conflict, and it is a way of illuminating the disingenuousness of the U.S. government's outlook.

Let us imagine two different peace processes. The first, the one that was embedded in Oslo and is described as the preferred future approach, rests on the notion that one leaves to the parties in conflict a framework within which to negotiate an outcome. That framework is embedded in the structure of geopolitics. It is the occupied against the occupier. It is the essence of translating power inequalities into politics. Negotiations under those circumstances—particularly with the United States standing in the background as the "facilitator," but in actuality that force that accentuates the power differential—rather than creating a balance in favor of the weaker side, reinforce existing inequities. Part of the way in which it accomplishes that is by excluding the relevance of international law and international humanitarian law.

This becomes clear if you imagine another peace process that would be guided in its framing of a just solution by the fundamental consensus as to the relevance of international law to several of the salient issues. For instance, there is no ambiguity about the right of Palestinian refugees to return as anchored firmly in international law. There is no question that the Security Council mantra, recited in resolutions 242 and 338, mandates withdrawal from the territory occupied in 1967. Furthermore, there is no question that the construction of the settlements is a flagrant, continuing, and direct violation of the third Geneva Convention governing occupation. Finally, there is no question that Jerusalem would be a city either shared or internationalized by reference to the pre-1967 realities.

If a peace process allowed international law to be relevant, it would indeed lead to a just outcome, or a relatively just outcome, which would put aside the relevance of inequalities in power and diplomatic leverage. One way to reach toward a meaningful peace process is to insist upon the relevance of international law and international humanitarian law, and to allow the argument made during the Oslo years to persist. That argument stated that any Palestinian grievances under international law would be dealt with in the final status negotiations. To raise those grievances otherwise, even by reference to clear international law, was to be disruptive of the peace process. Rather than to be part of the peace process, the relevance of international law was successfully put in the odd position of being an obstacle to peace.

It is a very perverse kind of inversion of what should be the fundamental guidelines and framework for a real peace process. One should realize in calling for adherence to international humanitarian law, which essentially means the Geneva Conventions and the more broad mandates of behavior that have been supported by the UN's more-or-less unanimous decisions, one is not calling for some idealistic or utopian set of standards to be applied. International humanitarian law represents a status compromise between the pursuit of military necessity and security by states, and minimal protections for civilian populations and occupied peoples. It is not a maximalist horizon of what justice might require for the Palestinian people, but it is at least a minimum benchmark of an outcome that is not completely dominated by geopolitics and the unequal, asymmetric power of the two sides.

It is important to keep these two images in mind, but it is also important to realize two things. One, the Palestinian leadership bears some of the responsibility for the failure to stress this dimension of their situation. They have been very reluctant, for instance, to allow the parties to the Geneva Convention to convene and carry out their own obligations, one of those being to see that the convention is implemented. It is a duty of the parties to do that, and there was a consensus of support for such a meeting, but Israel put pressure on Washington, and Washington put pressure on the Palestinians saying that this would not be useful. The Palestinians were told that this would divert attention from the prospects of successful negotiations.

It is all part of the ethos that you cannot talk about international rights and international law because that challenges Israel's willingness to proceed diplomatically. Israel's precondition for a peace process is an insistence that the United States, rather than the UN or Scandinavia, be the "dishonest broker" and that it is dysfunctional or immoral to invoke international law in framing just demands in the course of negotiations. What is unfortunate is that the Palestinian leadership has, to a confusing extant, acquiesced with these unreasonable conditions.

It is very costly, and not only in terms of how one envisions a just and fair solution. It has also enabled Israel, over the course of the occupation, to create "facts on the ground." It has altered the starting points of negotiation and, therefore, confused what a reasonable compromise should be. Through the cumulative illegality of the construction of settlements and of the Israelization of Jerusalem, the content of Palestinian self-determination has been severely impaired.

This reality is not static, but dynamic. Suspending the critical scrutiny that insists international law must be upheld in the course of the occupation—that every single settlement is a violation and inexcusable—has been a severe tactical mistake on the part of the Palestinian leadership. That acquiescence, however, is part of the subjugation making the Palestinians' choices unattractive.

Without trying to give technical explanations, the main departures from international humanitarian law and international law are the following:

- The underlying failure to withdraw, as mandated by the UN Security Council, from the territories occupied in 1967.
- The consistent reliance on collective punishment of the Palestinian people, which has taken really grotesque forms in the course of the response to the second *intifada*. It has interfered with the Palestinians'

most basic life circumstances making it a daily ordeal to survive physically, mentally, and spiritually. Article 33 of the Geneva Convention makes it very clear that collective punishments, under any circumstances, are illegal and unacceptable.

- The massive settlement program, by-pass roads, and armed military protection of the Israeli settlements are in fundamental violation of article 49, paragraph 6, of the third Geneva Convention. It violates the underlying premise of a legitimate occupation, namely, that the occupier does not try to change the character of the society being occupied.

- The repeated recourse to political assassination which is, again, explicitly prohibited by the Geneva Conventions.

- The denial of fundamental economic and social rights relating to employment, trade, investment, the receipt of education, and minimal medical treatment. All of these violations are serious and have been well documented.

In looking at this record, sustained over such a long period of time, and at the suffering that the Palestinian people endure in the Occupied Territories, it is significant that the international community has essentially been impotent to enforce its own standards. This has induced despair in many moderate Palestinians who seek to avoid a violent approach to achieving their self-determination.

They see that despite having international law consistently and unambiguously on their side, it makes no difference. Either there is a lack of political will or the geopolitics is not in their favor, but the only way to achieve protection is through forcible self-reliance. Part of the cruelty of the occupation is to give the Palestinian people a choice essentially between surrender and violence. There is no opportunity to rely on a peaceful approach that would presuppose serious attention to the relevance of international law.

Contrast the way Libya and Iraq have been treated for much less persistent, and much less consequential, violations of international law. They have been subject to sanctions, and they have been isolated in the international community. Recall the treatment of South Africa during the apartheid period. The Palestinian people feel they are victims of the most pronounced double standard that exists in international society.

Taking international law seriously only when it corresponds with geopolitical priorities undermines any respect for law and morality in international life. It is very costly and it has relevance beyond the specifics of this conflict. The United States bears a huge responsibility for this cynical manipulation of international humanitarian law, especially in circumstances where a people has been denied its fundamental right of self-determination.

If we seek a peace process that has some reasonable prospect of producing a viable Palestinian state and that does justice to Palestinian claims of self-determination, it must occur within a framework of international law and it must occur, not as an outcome, but as integral to the process.

As long as that does not occur, a substantial portion of the Palestinian people will not accept a process that produces the sort of solution the second Camp David Accord was seeking to impose. This basically incorporated into the settlement many of the illegalities that had been achieved and ingrained in the Israeli occupation, substantially legitimizing the facts on the ground. That is an unacceptable basis for a durable and viable peace.

Richard Falk, emeritus professor of politics and international affairs at Princeton University, writes on international relations. He is the author of Human Rights Horizons; Religion and Humane Global Governance; U.S. Power and the Multinational Corporation; War and Change in World Politics; *and* The Political Economy of International Relations. *He also served as a member of the three-member Palestine Human Rights Inquiry Commission that reported to the UN Human Rights Commission in Geneva.*

U.S. Policy in the Middle East And Central Asia

Martha Kessler

former CIA Political Officer

Scott Ritter

Former UN Arms Inspector

Fox News Network Political, Military Affairs Analyst

Glynn Wood

Professor, Monterey Institute of International Studies

Marwan Bishara

Fellow, Ecole de Hautes Etudes en Sciences Sociale

The United States
And Syria

by Martha Kessler

S yria is one of the most underestimated factors in the political dynamics of the Middle East. The relationship between the United States and Syria is perhaps the least examined in the Arab world. Washington has moderate Arab friends (Egypt, Jordan, Saudi Arabia, and the Gulf States) and it has enemies (Iran, Iraq, and Libya) all of which have received a great deal of energy and attention because of their direct connections to our interests. The other states in the region receive far less official examination, largely because they are not regarded as directly impacting our interests. Most American policymakers seems to have put Syria into this category, and thus U.S.-Syrian relations have had a discontinuous quality to them, jolted episodically by revitalized interest in the Arab-Israeli conflict and resolving it, and by our concerns over terrorism.

Unlike others who have been largely ignored by Washington, Syria seems to seek a position in America's peripheral vision, preferring to deal with European states rather than Washington. Syria has invested virtually nothing in cultivating the American foreign policy establishment fairly assiduously courted by other Arab governments. This odd mix of inattention on our part and seeming indifference on theirs has resulted in American perceptions and policies towards Syria that have been largely molded by Israel and other Syrian detractors.

Three decades of Hafez al-Assad's rule in Syria have lulled many into the view that this is a region anchored by a very stable and relatively predictable Syria. The repercussions on its neighbors of Syria degenerating into a failed state, or of a Muslim brotherhood coming to power in Damascus, are scenarios that have not really been played out in 20 years. Even as Assad's health was quite obviously failing him, it was clear to most observers that he had meticulously planned for his own passing, having groomed his son for leadership, installed a younger generation in key positions, and sidelined potential troublemakers and old school thinkers as best he could.

But more than a year has passed, and Bashar al-Assad's honeymoon period is over. The script that Hafez al-Assad and his son probably developed together could not have foreseen the events of 11 September and their effect on the region. Rather than attempt to predict Syria's future course, we should examine its attitude toward the United States and America's paramount interest in the war on terrorism. Those interests lie in the resolution of the peace process—that is, the resolution of the conflict between Israel and the Arab states—and in the region's stability, which is of paramount interest to the United States.

I will begin with my best understanding of Syria's view of relations with the United States which, at least in emphasis, varies quite considerably from the conventional characterization. The senior Assad seemed to see the collapse of the Soviet Union coming well before the rest of the world tuned in, or at least he foresaw the deterioration of state power tilting the world balance very much in favor of the United States. The importance of Moscow as Syria's patron rested not so heavily in the Soviet Union being a guarantor of the Assad regime, but in the superpowers containing the destructive potential of the Arab-Israeli conflict as part of their own balance of power.

The prospect of Moscow being unable to manage this task brought about one of the most dramatic shifts in Syrian policy during Assad's long tenure. After a nearly ten-year break with Egypt, Assad began to mend fences with Cairo as a prelude to working through the Egyptians to improve relations with the United States. This process was incremental and episodic, and the steps were subtle, but in a matter of years Syria reshaped its posture from a so-called Soviet surrogate, to a sought-after member of the American coalition in the Gulf War.

This transformation was critical to Assad's post-Soviet security posture for

Syria, which had as its centerpiece Syria's reliance on Washington to contain what is perceived by the Syrians as Israel's expansionist impulses, and to curtail its use of a vastly superior military capability on its Arab neighbors, specifically Syria. This new reliance required Syria to develop and maintain reasonable relationships with Washington, or stated another way, that Syria set a solid floor beneath which it would not allow U.S.-Syrian relations to drop. From Assad's perspective, Washington and Damascus did not need to see eye-to-eye on all regional issues, and Syria did not need to compromise its principles with regard to the return of the Golan Heights or the Palestinian issue in order to placate the United States. Syria did, however, need to convince American policymakers in one administration after another that Syria did not seek the destruction of Israel and was prepared to negotiate and honor a settlement of the dispute.

To that end, Assad made significant progress. He halted Syrian support to any form of international terrorism in the mid-eighties, worked to build effective ties with Egypt and Saudi Arabia—America's chief Arab friends—and made adjustments to satisfy America's concerns about Syrian and Lebanese involvement in the cultivation and movement of narcotics. He continued indirectly to allow, and to use, Hezbollah and other terrorist organizations in the struggle with Israel, but reined them in when Syria's safety appeared threatened or when American red-lines were in jeopardy of being crossed. Assad was the only Arab leader to vigorously defend Palestinian and Lebanese rights to combat Israel, articulating a rationale that the United States *de facto* accepted by incorporating the concept of red-lines and conflict protocols in most of its negotiations, particularly with regard to southern Lebanon.

While U.S.-Syrian relations throughout the last three American administrations were never warm, close, or even correct, that was never Assad's goal. He wanted the United States to see no justification for Israel undertaking military action, even on a limited scale, against Syria, and in that he was quite successful.

If the collapse of the Soviet Union and the end of superpower politics gave rise to Syria's new security posture, the decade of unsuccessful peace negotiations begun at the Madrid Conference confirmed for the Syrians the necessity of American management of Israel. Syria, like many other Arab states, believes Israel is an expansionist state with a dangerously factious and racist population that democratically produces weak governments. In the ten years of the Madrid negotiations, Assad, his family, and his colleagues watched the Israeli political leadership swing wildly from left to right, producing six prime ministers. They saw the only Israeli leader, in their view, seemingly capable of delivering what he negotiated gunned down by an internal dissident. They concluded that as Israel weakened politically, it had become even more dangerous militarily.

While Americans view the Madrid chapter of peace negotiations as a near miss of success, and now play the blame game as to why opportunities were lost, Hafez and, presumably, Bashar al-Assad have asked vastly different questions. But the importance of the United States managing Israel and remaining deeply engaged in the region has been proved unequivocally correct in Syrian eyes.

Despite my recent analytic energy looking for possible differences between the two, it is in fact not certain that father and son in the Assad family see the world and Syria's course in it exactly the same way. So far Bashar has shown a tentative tactical approach, but not a strategic purpose for those tactics different from his father's. It is probably too soon to make any pronouncements about his attitudes and plans for U.S.-Syrian relations, but his behavior toward Washington, his treatment of American diplomats, and his public pronouncements are similar to his father's *modus operandi*.

Bashar is certainly not the formidable leadership presence that Assad was when his life ended. The younger Assad faces remnants of a very old guard that resists any change touching its interests, and a young elite that seeks a complicated mix of change and stability, modernity and tradition. Bashar, like his father, must deal with ambitious relatives and corrupt ones, whom Hafez al-Assad could never bring himself to quash completely. Bashar's task of consolidating power will heavily influence the steps he takes in the near future, and we can expect expediency to prevail over principle as long as this task is ahead of him rather than behind him. By this measure, Bashar will need a cooperative relationship with the United States to stabilize the region so that he can build a durable structure within Syria. This is not the time for his fledgling regime to tackle the serious differences between Syria and the United States.

Turning to Syria's position in the peace process, the war on terrorism, and stability, if the senior Assad's position still holds, Syria's strategic goals in the peace arena are simple. Israel must return all the land it occupied in 1967 in return for a strong security regime and Arab guarantees of Israel's future. On the face of it, this vision offers little, if anything, more than America's articulated policy. This policy was heard many times, but is heard far less now—that the seizure of land by force is illegal and, hence, Israel's settlements are not recognized as legitimate and all sides must come to an agreement that guarantees the safety and security of all.

In the years since the 1973 war, prior to which these views were last clearly articulated, America's original position has been suborned to its role as a negotiator. It has been watered down and obfuscated to provide maximum diplomatic flexibility, so that we now stand for no more than accepting whatever the two parties can agree to. American diplomatic efforts, no matter how artful and persevering, are no substitute for vision and leadership, and we trade principles for diplomatic agility. As a consequence, we have produced process, but absolutely no results. The Syrians had hoped that the Madrid Conference would work, but that hope was fleeting and only existed around the period when they were negotiating with Rabin. There is essentially a sense that negotiations are probably not in their interest at this time, as long as Bashar still needs to build his internal power base, and that there are real wild cards out there that could make negotiations dangerous. Like all of the other countries of the region, Syria has been deeply affected by the violence of the *intifada,* which has enraged the Syrian public, and there is likely to be a rethinking of Syria's reclusiveness in response to pressure from the Syrian public.

Syria's attitude toward negotiations on the Palestinian issue is that the tortured interaction between the Syrian leadership and the Palestinian leadership had, as a defining twist, Assad's bitter judgment that Oslo was a terrible tactical mistake by Yasser Arafat—a mistake that all would come to regret and pay for. Syria's recent efforts to tie its negotiating future more closely to the Palestinians is, paradoxically, an attempt to showcase the rightness of Assad's prediction and to inhibit any new freelancing by Arafat.

Anticipating a hiatus before returning to the negotiating table, the chief planners of Syrian policy—Bashar and Foreign Minister al-Shara'—do not have a highly articulated plan for the resumption of talks, apart from commencing any new effort on the firm basis of the terms of reference (TORs) originally designed for the Madrid Conference. The key feature of these TORs is the explicit commitment of all parties to UN resolutions 242 and 338 as the basis for negotiations.

Syria has always sought to wrap itself in international law, and has approached the peace process completely unwilling to step away from this. While one can reasonably argue that they have made no advances, the Syrians believe that their position remains intact and they would like to see the Palestinians pursue a similar course.

Martha Kessler has worked with the CIA on the Middle East and South Asia for the last 30 years. She has held positions throughout the Directorate of Intelligence and served three tours in the National Intelligence Council. She was a senior fellow at the National Defense University and was a guest scholar at the Brookings Institution, where she wrote a number of studies on the Middle East and the peace process, some of which have been published in Middle East Policy. *She is currently completing another book on Syria.*

Understanding the Roots of Terrorism:
Iraq as a Case Study

by Scott Ritter

When we talk about understanding the roots of terrorism, we need to be more specific. We are talking about understanding the roots of those who perpetrated the 11 September attacks, and using that as a model for future acts of terror against the United States or American-type targets.

Let us start off by saying that those who perpetrated this crime did not do this out of sympathy for the Iraqi people. They did not do this out of solidarity with Saddam Hussein. They did this because, frankly speaking, their militancy in the name of Islam led them to perpetrate a horrible crime against humanity. We should not focus on the terrorists who perpetrated the crime, but rather, what about American foreign policy helped motivate them.

People are not born to commit crimes. People are not born to commit acts of terror. It is an evolutionary process. What is it about America's policies that compels people to evolve towards terror, evolve towards committing crimes which, when one considers the peaceful character of the Islamic religion, fly in the face of the very cause these criminals purport to support? So again, let us not talk about a direct link between Iraq and the terrorists. This is not something that is motivated by Saddam Hussein, but let us look at Iraq as a model upon which we can evaluate the larger question of what motivates people to have such deep seated anti-American sentiment that they might move in the direction of committing these crimes.

Iraq is probably one of the most effective models of American unilateralist policies. It is this policy of unilateralism that alienates the United States from much of the world today. To give an example, when I speak to university or high school students, or church or religious groups, I throw out the name Iraq and ask people to respond with the first thing that comes to mind. The vast majority of people generally say Saddam Hussein. The concept that we can characterize a nation as complex as Iraq with the identity of a single individual is in itself indicative of some of the problems we have in dealing with the Middle East as a region, as a culture, etc.

The United States is singularly focused on one man in Iraq, and that is Saddam Hussein. We have built policies that seek to minimize his ability to rule that country, minimize his ability to extend Iraq's influence outside of its borders, and ultimately to remove this man from power. In doing so we have come with a number of policy options. Most well known is the policy of disarming Iraq and removing Iraq's weapons of mass destruction, but we should be very frank and honest about this. The United States supported resolution 687 in April 1991 not because they really cared about Iraq's weapons of mass destruction. That was secondary. It was because the resolution provided a vehicle for containing, destabilizing, and ultimately removing Saddam Hussein from power.

From the very start, the decade-long track record of the failure of America's policy towards Iraq, there is a contradictory divergence in the way America deals with Iraq. On the one hand is the basis of international law, the Security Council resolutions passed under Chapter 7 of the UN Charter, calling for Iraq's disarmament. Disarming Iraq is what the international community has agreed to. On the other hand is America's unilateral policy of destabilizing and overthrowing Saddam Hussein. Carefully read all the resolutions that talk about Iraq's disarmament. None of them link disarmament to Saddam Hussein's removal from power. Saddam Hussein is not part of this equation, except in the minds of American policymakers. First and foremost in America's mindset is the removal of Saddam Hussein and resolution 687 was part and parcel of the overall creation of a policy designed to destabilize and ultimately remove this man from power.

This did not work. In 1991, James Baker and Richard Haas, who is now director of policy planning at the State Department, said that no one expected Hussein to last more than six months. The disarmament process was always expected to last more than six months, so the formulation was that once Hussein was gone, whoever replaced him would cooperate with the weapons inspectors and those weapons would be gone. But we would have succeeded in our policy of getting rid of Hussein because getting rid of this man is really all that American policymakers care about.

Why would they want to get rid of him? Why is it such a singularity? That is another cornerstone of the American problem vis-à-vis the Middle East—American domestic politics. In terms of going to war with Iraq in 1990-91, Saddam Hussein was sold to the American public as the personification of evil, the Middle East equivalent of Adolph Hitler. This was a war not about the liberation of Kuwait, or guaranteeing supplies of oil to the American economy, but rather good versus evil with America the embodiment of good and Saddam Hussein the embodiment of evil. We were taking on the evildoers, and if people catch a ring of parallelism between what happened in 1991 with what is happening today, that is done on purpose. It is clearly a reflection of the kind of unilateral policies we carry out, a living embodiment of unilateralism.

Having quantified this conflict as good versus evil, Saddam Hussein's continued survival makes it virtually impossible for American policymakers to do anything other than continuously confront this dictator. By describing the conflict in black and white terms of good versus evil, you take out an entire range of options in the gray areas in the middle that one could seek toward a resolution of this issue.

Saddam Hussein's continued survival meant that. Disarmament and economic sanctions did not work, and so we had to have other factors to contain him. The so-called "no-fly zones" are another aspect of America's policy toward Iraq. These no-fly zones were ostensibly created for humanitarian purposes—to defend the Kurds in the north and the Shi'a in the south—but American warplanes have never dropped a bomb in defense of the Kurdish people or the Shi'a. The United States never will because this is Orwellian doublespeak.

We talk about our sympathy for the Kurds, but we do not care about the Kurds. We talk about our sympathy for the Shi'a, but we do not care about the Shi'a. We care about the Sunni in Baghdad who will retain the reins of power as long as our focus on Iraq is on getting access to Iraqi oil. We do not want democracy in Iraq because if Iraq had democracy, the Shi'a would dominate. The Shi'a then would be feared because they would lean towards Iran. That is not what we want, but we talk about it. It is doublespeak.

It is all about Saddam. And our enforcement of these no-fly zones is not humanitarian. It is to secure Turkey's borders, to secure Kuwait's borders, and to destabilize Saddam Hussein. It is also a gross violation of international law. There is no Security Council resolution that provides any basis for the continued enforcement of the no-fly zone. And yet, in another failure of American policy, we do it and state that we do so for humanitarian reasons backed by the Security Council.

Now, what are the ramifications and the impact of this policy? Saddam Hussein still reigns in Baghdad today. There is no viable hope of removing him from power. The cost of our policy, however, while it has not impacted Hussein, has had a terrible impact on the people of Iraq due to the ongoing economic sanctions. The ongoing isolation engendered by this American-dominated policy of focusing on Hussein has killed between 500,000 to 1.2 million people, mainly children and the elderly, the sick and the weakest—the very ones the UN is supposed to be protecting are suffering.

Now what does this mean? Again, the 11 September terrorists did not act out of solidarity with Saddam Hussein or with the Iraqi people. But when you take a look at the model of American policy towards Iraq, you see that America's unilateral policy objectives will always take precedence over the international community's policy objectives—i.e., disarming Iraq versus removing Saddam Hussein. The removal of Saddam Hussein is first and foremost.

International law will be manipulated, abused, and indeed violated, when it suits America's unilateral policy objectives, such as the enforcement of the no-fly zones.

We may talk about sympathies with people. We may talk about how much we feel the pain of the Iraqi people. But 500,000 to 1.2 million of them have died, and this brings up one of the more controversial points about America's Middle East policy. Our policymakers do not wake up in the morning and say, "Look, we are going to have a racist policy today. We are going to go out and persecute the Middle East people because they are not white like us." But the fact of the matter is we would never allow 500,000 French children to starve to death. We would never allow 500,000 British children to starve to death. We would never even allow 500,000 Serbian children to starve to death. The fact that these are Iraqis has no significance in the minds of Americans, and the same holds true in the cases of Afghans, Sudanese, Egyptians, Saudis, and Iranians.

If you want to talk about the roots of terror, talk about the suffering of people in the Middle East who have to exist under corrupt regimes supported by the United States. America will continue to support these regimes because of its own unilateral policy objective of creating stable access to oil. This is the route of terror, not necessarily Iraq, but the model of American pursuit of foreign policy objectives leading millions of people to live in abject poverty with no hope whatsoever of a better future. And, therefore, they gravitate toward extremism, they gravitate toward militancy, they gravitate toward terror.

Scott Ritter worked in military intelligence during an extensive and distinguished career in the U.S. Armed Forces, with assignments in the Soviet Union and the Middle East. He is a former Major in the U.S. Marine Corps and he spent several months during the Gulf War serving under General Schwartzkopf at his headquarters in Saudi Arabia.

U.S. Policy
In Pakistan and Afghanistan

by Glynn Wood

P rior to 11 September, American policy in South Asia was a tale of three major Cold War initiatives taken by the United States that had major consequences for the region. All three were taken in the spirit of a crusade, for principles thought to transcend purely national interest, and in each case the goal was to protect the free world from communist domination. Envisioned was a new world order which would supplant the old colonial order that had managed world affairs prior to World War II. These initiatives were taken with the Wilsonian spirit that has alternated uncomfortably in American foreign policy with a spirit of continental isolation, best expressed by Washington in his farewell address when he warned against "entangling foreign alliances."

For the new nations of South Asia (and the older nation of Afghanistan), colonialism left unfinished business with the Partition of 1947. Particularly difficult was the sorting out of the contested boundaries left behind by the British, and in that unstable environment each Cold War initiative would quickly demonstrate the wisdom of Tip O'Neill's axiom, "All politics is local some place."

That the troubled relationship between Pakistan and Afghanistan is as old as the creation of Pakistan was clearly demonstrated when Pakistan applied for admission to the UN. The new nation was welcomed by all members except

Afghanistan, whose delegate cast the single negative vote. That vote signaled Afghanistan's rejection of the Durand line, a British colonial artifact that divided the Pashtu-speaking people who inhabit both southern Afghanistan and Pakistan's Northwest Frontier Province (NWFP). During the struggle for independence, Nehru and Gandhi's Congress party had had considerable support in the NWFP, unlike the rest of West Pakistan. Their leader in the province was Ghaffar Khan, known as the "Frontier Gandhi," and he and his supporters opposed the partitioning of colonial India. But when the new boundaries were drawn in 1947, Khan's party found themselves stranded in Pakistan. Many of Khan's Pashtu-speaking followers joined a movement for a free Pashtunistan, a movement that had the sympathy and covert support of the Afghan government.

The Afghan government of King Zahir Shah, managed by his cousin Prime Minister Daud, did its best over the next 25 years to interest the rest of the world in the Pashtunistan issue, but Pashtunistan was just one on a long list of would-be nations claiming justice for their cause as European colonialism was losing its grip. For Mohammed Ali Jinnah's new government in Pakistan, the Pashtunistan issue was simply subversion and an attempt to discredit Pakistan's claim to be the homeland for all South Asian Muslims. In addition, the Pashtunistan threat on his northwest border was a major distraction from Pakistan's real challenge, the hostile India that was a wedge between East and West Pakistan.

Both parties to the Pashtunistan quarrel shopped around for international support. Here the United States first appears on the scene in the first of three major Cold War initiatives. In each case American policies were explained and justified in terms that transcended narrow national interest, but the actions taken were soon entangled with local concerns. Within South Asia, these American initiatives invariably provided either opportunities or threats for players intent on advancing their national concerns, and in each case the broader international issue quickly became entangled with regional agendas producing consequences that had little to do with international communism as such. This paper will describe those three initiatives and their consequences, before turning to the current crisis centered in Afghanistan and New York City.

Initiative I. Containing Communism: The security alliances

When John Foster Dulles negotiated the first round of security treaties for the region in 1954, his goal was to create an alliance of non-Communist states that would make up a "Northern Tier" of states that could block any Communist incursion into the Near East and South Asia. In his initial plan, both India and Pakistan were to be key players in a phalanx that would run from Turkey to East Pakistan. Generous military and economic resources were on offer to partners who joined the alliances.

When Dulles announced his plan for defending the region, one of the first countries to request assistance was Afghanistan. The Afghan government knew that its military badly needed modernization and that American assistance seemed the best available. However, when Dulles turned down the Afghan request on the grounds that Afghanistan belonged within the Soviet sphere of influence, Prime Minister Daud moved on to his second choice. The Soviet Union agreed to take on the job of modernization and their advisors and equipment were brought in for a major program of assistance that did upgrade Afghan military capacity while placing that portion of the Afghan government truly within the Soviet sphere of influence.

The major gap in Dulles' plan for a grand alliance occurred when India refused to join. Although Nehru had recently put down a Communist insurrection in south India, he argued that security alliances would infringe on the national sovereignty that the Indians had so recently won. Instead, he was in the process of committing himself and India to a position of non-alignment that he hoped would allow India and other post-colonial nations to avoid building up their militaries while remaining outside the Cold War struggle.

On the other hand, Pakistan saw the Dulles offer as an opportunity to upgrade a military that was still smarting from the stalemate that had ended Pakistan's first war with India, a stalemate that had left most of the disputed territory of Kashmir in Indian hands. A deal was struck, and Pakistan became a member of both the Baghdad Pact (CENTO) and the South East Asia Treaty Organization (SEATO). The assistance received then allowed Pakistan to embark on a major military modernization program directed by General Ayub Khan, the same general who in 1958 would lead the coup d'etat that created Pakistan's first military government.

During the initial stages of the CENTO-SEATO relationship with the United States, Pakistan did greatly increase its military capacity, but in retrospect it seems unlikely that its membership in those alliances made it any less vulnerable to Communist threats. Certainly in one instance, the partnership placed Pakistan in direct nuclear jeopardy. As part of the agreement, the United States was allowed to use the Pakistani air base in Peshawar to send U-2s on their surveillance flights over the Soviet Union. Pakistan's risk became quite clear in 1960, when Gary Powers' U-2 was shot down while flying over the Soviet Union. In the aftermath an enraged Khruschev directly threatened Pakistan with nuclear retaliation, a threat taken quite seriously by the Pakistanis.

Within the region, the results of the alliance were also obvious, for both India and Afghanistan objected to a program that threatened to alter the military balance in the region. For the Afghans this objection was more than theoretical, in that the Pakistanis used American planes and ordnance when bombing and strafing Pathan insurgents in the tribal areas of the NWFP, insurgents who were committed to a free Pashtunistan.

This low-grade insurgency continued in the NWFP for the next 25 years, but for Afghanistan (and India) the Cold War had taken a different turn by 1960. While threatening Pakistan for its alignment, Khruschev softened Soviet foreign policy to allow friendship and support for what the Soviets called progressive (i.e., not overtly anti-Communist) governments. As non-aligned countries, both Afghanistan and India became recipients of Soviet economic assistance, and much to Pakistan's chagrin, the United States began to counter the Soviet offers with matching programs of assistance for the non-aligned.

Now the competition of East and West became an economic and psychological contest in which both sides of the Cold War attempted to demonstrate their friendship for the non-aligned and the superiority of their respective systems through cooperative projects and rather heavy-handed propaganda. In Afghanistan, both the United States and the Soviet Union became heavily involved in building roads and schools, in a country that had previously had very few of either.

For the Pakistanis this turn of events devalued their partnership with the United States. Both her unfriendly neighbors were receiving benefits similar to theirs, without facing any nuclear threat. The invidious comparisons made with their non-aligned neighbors were damaging to U.S.-Pakistani relations, but worse was in store for both Pakistan and India.

Initiative II. Meeting the Chinese communist threat

Nehru's rejection of the Western security alliances was a major step in the creation of what would become the Non-Aligned Movement (NAM), but his commitment to the non-alignment principles set forth at the Bandung conference in 1956 could not withstand the challenges India faced in the 1960s. In 1962 India's own non-alignment policy was destroyed by the Sino-Indian war.

While India and China had been partners in establishing the NAM at Bandung, soon afterward they found themselves at odds over the Sino-Indian border inherited from the colonial period. Their conflict also produced a major contradiction troubling for anyone committed to opposing monolithic Communism, for India was under attack from a Communist country, while receiving both military and economic assistance from the Soviets. As the Sino-Indian crisis escalated, the Soviet Union continued its assistance programs, which included the sale and eventual production of Soviet MIG fighters in India. But when war actually broke out in October 1962, the Soviets managed to avoid direct opposition to the Chinese by taking a neutral position on the conflict and by slowing down the flow of military supplies to India.

The cautious neutrality of the Soviets contrasted sharply with President Kennedy's quick and enthusiastic response to Nehru's request for help. American war materiel was delivered within a week of Nehru's request, and the U.S. Military Assistance Group (USMAG) established at that time continued to work with the Indian military even after the Chinese announced a unilateral cease-fire. For more than two years the USMAG in New Delhi undermined any claim of non-alignment that India could make.

That American support of India continued after the cease-fire that ended the Sino-Indian war was an alarming development for the Pakistanis. Even though the USMAG in Pakistan continued its assistance program, that assistance was being matched by the USMAG in India that was continuing to build up the Indian military to counter the Chinese threat. Obviously India's improved capacity was equally available for any India-Pakistan conflict, and, in addition, the whole episode had demonstrated that an aligned Pakistan took no precedence over a non-aligned India when South Asia was threatened by Communist aggression. Pakistan's response was to strengthen its relationship with China—a relationship extremely useful for both parties as they continued their disputes with India. In the end, both USMAGs were heavy contributors to an arms race that ended with the Indo-Pakistan war of 1965.

That war provides an ironic demonstration of superpower intentions running headlong into regional interests, for both armies used their American Cold War assistance to settle their regional dispute. The two USMAGs found themselves in the line of fire when war broke out in the Punjab and Kashmir in August. The American response to this unintended and unauthorized use of military assistance was to place an arms embargo on the whole region that was not lifted for ten years.

The 1965 war was short-lived and indecisive, with a cease-fire called after only a month of fighting. During that month the United States had offended both adversaries with the arms embargo. The Soviet Union, on the other hand, managed to avoid taking sides, which then allowed Soviet President Kosygin to serve as an honest broker at the peace conference in Tashkent, the conference where he personally was able to negotiate the agreement that formally ended the war.

From the Pakistani perspective, the 1965 war conclusively demonstrated the limited value of their security alliances with the United States. Those alliances might be helpful against hypothetical Communist aggression, but were of little use in dealing with the real threats Pakistan faced within the region. The formal alliances (CENTO and SEATO) would continue for a time, but the American failure to provide assistance when Pakistan really needed it in 1965 convinced them that the alliances had little value.

In the years that followed the 1965 war American policy toward South Asia can best be described as benign neglect. America's involvement in Southeast Asia left little surplus for major initiatives in South Asia. President Nixon did find Pakistan a useful ally in negotiating his opening to China, but his widely publicized "tilt" toward Pakistan during the Bangladesh crisis made little difference when Pakistan was partitioned for the second time. Globally, this was also the period of détente, with considerable reduction in East-West tensions through bilateral negotiations across a range of issues, a positive trend that ended abruptly in 1979 when the Soviets invaded Afghanistan.

Initiative III. Meeting the Soviet threat

The Carter administration was ill-prepared for the Soviet invasion of Afghanistan in December of 1979. Carter's administration was deeply involved in the Embassy hostage crisis in Iran when reports of the Soviet Army rolling south came in. Carter and his advisors were truly shocked and they became Cold War warriors overnight, embarking on a major program to thwart what was seen as an outrageous act of Communist aggression. With the advantage of hindsight the Russian invasion might better be described as a Soviet effort to suppress a brutal regime run by Afghan Communists whose radical program of reform had little to do with Communist doctrine as that doctrine was understood in Moscow.

Afghanistan's Communist regime had come to power 20 months before in a coup organized by the Afghan Communist party, the People's Democratic Party of Afghanistan (PDPA). The government displaced by the PDPA had been an authoritarian left-leaning republic headed by Sardar Daud, cousin and brother-in-law to King Zahir Shah, whose constitutional monarchy Daud had overthrown five years before. In both coups, leftist military officers had played a major role, and there is some evidence of Soviet support for both coups. But neither coup received much attention in an America still recovering from the Vietnam War and much more concerned internationally with oil, nuclear weapons, and the hostages in Tehran.

Within Afghanistan, the period of PDPA rule was turbulent indeed. In all the many accounts of the 20 months during which their government ran Afghanistan, the key player was Hafizullah Amin. Amin, who had pursued doctoral studies at Columbia University, was initially foreign minister in the first government named by the PDPA's Revolutionary Council. That council appointed a writer named Nur Mohammed Taraki as both president and prime minister. Once in office, Taraki found Amin to be his most useful colleague, and he was first promoted to deputy prime minister and then given the prime ministership when President Taraki gave up that position. Amin's program for reforming the Afghan economy and society was both broad-based and radical. When those reforms were resisted by conservative Afghans, Amin's security forces responded with a harshness that quickly gave the regime a reputation for excessive brutality.

The regime's repression set off a cycle of violence that shocked its Soviet advisors and eventually President Taraki decided that Amin had to go. A confrontation in the president's office ended in a shootout, but Amin escaped and managed to have Taraki arrested and killed. Meanwhile, the Soviets had decided to acknowledge the regime as a legitimate Communist state. With that recognition came strong criticism of the Amin government's performance. Amin paid little heed to Soviet criticism, and at least two attempts on his life failed. Then in December of 1979 the Soviet Army marched in, and during the struggle for Kabul, Amin was killed. The Soviet's choice, Babrak Karmal, was brought out of exile to become the new President.

For the Carter administration this was a call to arms, and a classic proxy war ensued, with Afghan rebels supported by the United States and all of the Islamic world. The Reagan administration was an even stronger supporter of Afghan insurgents. In this proxy war the key player was Pakistan, then led by the military dictator General Zia ul Haq. Until the Soviet invasion General Zia's government had received little sympathy from a Carter administration that placed great emphasis on democratic rule and human rights, both in short supply in Pakistan. In addition, Pakistan was still under an American arms embargo and its nuclear program was suspected of developing nuclear weapons counter to American non-proliferation policy.

These concerns evaporated as the United States put together plans to support the Afghan rebels, and after considerable bargaining by General Zia, Pakistan became *the* front-line state in a struggle that continued until the last Soviet troops were withdrawn in February 1989. For its contribution, Pakistan negotiated a succession of large military and economic aid packages from the United States in exchange for its support of the Afghan mujahidin. American assistance was supplemented by both private and governmental funds from the oil rich countries in the Middle East, who also sympathized with the Afghan rebels.

During the nearly ten years of fighting Afghanistan was devastated. A million Afghans were killed and some five million refugees fled the country. Almost half of those refugees ended up in Pakistan, either in refugee camps along the northern border or in Pakistani cities.

In their fight with the Soviets, the mujahidin had the assistance of Pakistan's Inter-Service Intelligence Agency (ISI), which provided arms and training for the rebels, while expanding rebel ranks by bringing in volunteers from Pakistan and other Muslim countries. In the process, the Pakistani military was able to upgrade their own military capacity which helped compensate for their previous difficulties with the American arms embargo. In addition, Pakistan's alliance with the rebels ended, for the time being, any kind of Pashtunistan threat, for most Pathans were grateful for Pakistan's assistance.

The results of Pakistan's front-line performance went beyond military operations. In the process of giving safe haven to both Afghan rebels and refugees, Pakistani society was greatly changed. The Islamic schools set up at Saudi expense produced a generation of students *(talib)* who were instructed in a radical version of Islam. They also became available for the street demonstrations that are a major tactic for Pakistan's Islamic parties.

In addition, the refugees, whether in camps along the northwestern frontier or in Pakistan's cities, were high maintenance—especially in the cities where Afghans became involved in inter-ethnic strife. While the cost of refugee maintenance was originally covered by the external funding provided for the war effort, when the Soviets withdrew from Afghanistan international support for the refugees was greatly reduced, and more refugees came to escape the turmoil that followed Soviet withdrawal.

The impact of Gorbachev's decision to pull out of Afghanistan undercut the logic of superpower confrontation, while at the same time reducing American interest in the region. Then with the breakup of the Soviet Union, the newly independent Central Asian republics became the custodians of Afghanistan's northern frontier, and Cold War conflict in the region was over. As a result, neither the first Bush administration nor the Clinton administration would see Afghanistan as a high priority, and although both were involved in Afghanistan's peace negotiations in Geneva, the third major American initiative had ended. So begins another period of benign neglect, a period that would end on 11 September 2001.

Initiative IV. Meeting the terrorism threat

In President Bush's call for a worldwide campaign against terrorism, no country is more important or more problematic than Pakistan, and in entering that relationship Pakistan was all too aware that it had been thrice burned by earlier American initiatives. To date, President Pervez Musharraf has said all the right things in responding to President Bush's call for cooperation in ridding the world of terrorism and *al-Qaeda*. Musharraf sent a high level delegation to Afghanistan to deliver an American ultimatum to the Taliban regime in a final attempt to avoid war. That mission failed, but now that the fighting has begun, what else does Pakistan bring to the table? What will they expect in return? What risks are involved for Pakistan and the United States in this new alliance?

In his first televised speech to the Pakistani people after 11 September, Musharraf announced that he had agreed to support President Bush's efforts against terrorism with intelligence sharing, logistical support, and use of Pakistani air space.

Use of Pakistani air space and logistical support for any military operations in land-locked Afghanistan are Pakistan's most obvious assets. Pakistan's military bases are particularly helpful, for these are installations familiar to the American military, from their use during the Soviet-Afghan war. Of the six other immediate neighbors of Afghanistan, only Uzbekistan has gone beyond general support to offer logistical support for the American and British effort.

For the immediate goal of extricating bin Laden from his Afghan hideout, no country can match Pakistani intelligence resources because bin Laden's international warriors have long had close connections with Pakistan's ISI. Bin Laden and his men are the militants recruited from around the world to liberate Afghanistan from godless Communism, and in that struggle they were valued allies of the Afghan resistance. During that war ISI was the principal agency that delivered weapons and funds to the resistance—funds supplied mainly by the United States and Saudi Arabia.

In the chaos that ensued after the Russian withdrawal, bin Laden's militants did not go home. Instead they eventually aligned themselves with the Taliban movement which, by 1995, was finally able to restore law and order in most of Afghanistan. That pacification campaign was also supported by ISI, who found both the Taliban and bin Laden's group sympathetic to their major concern—supporting the insurgency under way in India-held Kashmir.

In his speech to the Pakistani people, Musharraf made it clear that his decision to support the Bush initiative was a difficult one, but that he believed it would help Pakistan extricate itself from a difficult position. As a general who came to power through a military coup, Musharraf is all too aware that Pakistan is vulnerable politically, economically, and militarily. On all three fronts, he expects to improve his chances by cooperating with the Bush initiative. Politically, he will expect less pressure to return Pakistan to civilian leadership; an end to the sanctions imposed by the United States because of his nuclear program; and a more favorable hearing in the international community for Pakistan's claims on the disputed territory of Kashmir.

Economically, Musharraf is badly in need of debt relief. Since taking power his government has been in continuous negotiation with the World Bank over terms of further loans, and those negotiations have been contentious. The result has been a tight leash on new credits, with only minimal grants designed to prevent financial collapse while Pakistan's past performance is reviewed and new terms negotiated. His signing on with the anti-terrorist alliance has already set off a series of loans and grants from the United States, Japan, and the International Monetary Fund (IMF).

Pakistan's financial crises and the international sanctions imposed after Pakistan tested its nuclear weapons have resulted in a military that is threadbare. The tests demonstrated Pakistan's nuclear capabilities, but also served to further impoverish her conventional forces. From this crisis, Musharraf certainly expects to receive more favorable terms for American and other weapons he needs in order to bring the Pakistani military up to current standards.

The risks for Pakistan in this joint effort are considerable, but this has been the case during previous partnerships. Already the Taliban regime has threatened *jihad* against Pakistan should they get involved in a military effort in Afghanistan. While the Taliban military has little offensive capability, the presence of three million Afghan refugees in Pakistan poses a considerable threat to domestic order, an order already threatened by feuding between violent factions within Pakistan. In addition, the militant Islamic party, *Jamaat-i-Islam,* opposes any cooperation with the United States, and while this party has had little success in Pakistani elections, it is capable of turning out street demonstrations that have been difficult for civil or military authorities to control.

Finally, Musharraf's ability to control his own military in this endeavor is not guaranteed. The loyalty of enlisted soldiers and younger officers will be tested by any military operations carried out against Islamic militants. Shortly after announcing his decision to join the alliance against terrorism, Musharraf replaced the head of ISI, along with the two other top generals who directed the coup that brought him to power. Musharraf described this change of leadership as routine, but it is likely to be a sign of dissent within the military establishment as well.

For the United States, there are also risks in working with this particular ally. The Pakistani ISI has long had the reputation of working independently of the formal policies pursued by the government in Islamabad. While ISI is best positioned to provide intelligence on bin Laden, and any other terrorist activity in Afghanistan, it is an organization that has its own goals, and ISI's primary objective since 1989 has been support for the militants in Kashmir. That support cannot be easily reconciled with their new task and this conflict of interest means that any intelligence supplied by ISI requires careful scrutiny.

A second risk for the United States is the impact any bargain made with Pakistan will have on America's relationship with India. The Indian government enthusiastically endorsed Bush's worldwide campaign against terrorism, and offered any support required for the American effort in Afghanistan. From India's perspective any campaign against terrorism would eventually target the Kashmiri insurgents. This means that almost any gains made by the Musharraf government in the anti-terrorism campaign will be seen as a blow to India's own security, so long as the insurgency in Kashmir continues.

Finally, for the United States and the world, the possible destabilization of the Pakistani government has become a matter of much greater concern since India and Pakistan demonstrated their nuclear capability in the summer of 1998. In his first reaction to those tests, President Clinton called South Asia "the most dangerous place in the world." That extreme reaction has abated somewhat over the last three years. Most discussions of South Asian nuclear weapons now focus on the more practical problems of nuclear safety and command and control rather than on intentional nuclear exchanges. Considerable confidence has been developed that the current military government of Pakistan, and any subsequent government run by Pakistan's current military establishment or by Pakistan's two major parties, would manage their nuclear weapons responsibly. That confidence would be shattered should a militant regime take over the government in reaction to this crisis.

In this fourth American initiative in South Asia President Bush is pursuing policies on terrorism that parallel policies other countries have attempted in a more limited fashion and with limited success. Whether this global effort can succeed will require that American policymakers deal with the regional concerns of South Asia. To date, the Afghan and Pakistani cases demonstrate just how difficult that task is going to be.

 *Glynn Wood, academic dean and provost of the Monterey Institute for International Studies from 1980-97, has also served as cultural officer for the United States Information Agency in Lebanon, Afghanistan, and India. He was a trainer for the Foreign Service Institute and a consultant on South Asian affairs for General Dynamics, Dupont, General Electric, and the United States Department of Defense.*

Asymmetric
Conflict

by Marwan Bishara

America's worst nightmare came true on Tuesday, 11 September 2001. Two of the super-power's most cherished symbols, the Pentagon and the World Trade Center, were hit, leading to the deaths of thousands and the loss of tens of billions of dollars in less than an hour. Paradoxically this came at a time when America had reinforced its "zero-dead" approach to future conflict—an approach calling for minimum casualties on the American side while inflicting maximum damage to the enemy.

President Bush declared America "at war" before identifying the enemy, promising a "crusade," or *"jihad,"* against the West's "evil" enemies. "It's Pearl Harbor," Americans remarked in the absence of adequate reference points. Unlike other opponents in the past century, this enemy is known chiefly for precisely what it is not—a state. The new enemy is mobile, transnational or sub-national, and deadly, said the commentators. Unlike Japan's attack on 7 December 1941, the terrorists who hit America were faceless actors with no legal address. There are primary suspects, but they are not accountable to UN charters or, for that matter, to any secular authority.

For decades, America has spent trillions of dollars to insure minimum casualties in any future confrontation. In the Vietnam War, America spent hundreds of thousands of dollars for each dead Vietnamese fighter. After spending trillions more over the following two decades, America succeeded in minimizing its own casualties in the Gulf War. Under the Powell Doctrine of rapid and massive bombardment from afar, America anticipated no casualties resulting from future symmetrical wars. Its cruise missiles and superior fighters, supported with the most sophisticated airborne intelligence, could guarantee such results by bringing unbearable destruction on the enemy, regardless of its casualties.

That is, until four commercial airplanes with full fuel tanks were transformed into high-explosive missiles by what appear to have been middle class hijackers using only knives and box cutters and willing to die for their cause. Nineteen of them died while killing thousands. This is not the sort of battle America is equipped to fight. Terrorism crossed the Atlantic skillfully and successfully, fulfilling America's own prophecy. Why?

This is just the sort of "asymmetric war" scenario some American strategists have been warning against for the last few years. America, the military and economic superpower, with a very low tolerance for casualties when it comes to civilian and military deaths, was hit where it would hurt most, in the symbols of its might, the Pentagon and Wall Street. The perpetrators succeeded mainly in terrorizing and tormenting "Main Street" America.

The new asymmetric threat

Once the Cold War put an end to symmetrical conflicts involving the almighty America—although Saddam Hussein did not realize this—Washington began to rethink its deterrence capacity and its ability to confront the new dangers to its national security and its interests abroad. The Revolution in Military Affairs (RMA) was introduced in the Pentagon within the context of an evolving globalization. Two distinct schools of thought emerged that were soon to converge under the junior Bush administration.

The first spoke of fourth-generation warfare, sometimes referred to as "stateless" or "asymmetric" warfare, which would be fought against an "opponent who might have a non-nation-state base, such as an ideology or religion." Central Intelligence Agency (CIA) Director George J. Tenet emphasized this in his 7 February 2001 statement before the Senate Select Committee on Intelligence, "Worldwide Threat 2001: National Security in a Changing World." He was struck most forcefully by "the accelerating pace of change in so many arenas that affect our nation's interests."

To the American mind, asymmetry alludes to the likes of bin Laden and other international terrorists, Mafias, and drug dealers. But it also encompassed non-state actors like those confronted in Somalia, Kosovo, and even Lebanon in the early 1980s when the Marine barracks was bombed. The proponents of this school of thought challenged the supporters of a business-as-usual approach to explain the point of spending billions of dollars on new fighter planes and advanced frigates when two men and a small boat could crash into the U.S.S. Cole, severely damaging it and killing 17 servicemen. They argued that advanced technology warfare is largely ineffective against terrorism and fourth-generation opponents.

The second camp concentrated on a missile defense shield that would protect America from incoming ballistic missiles carrying chemical, biological, or nuclear weapons. This was a watered-down version of Reagan's "Star Wars," but it nonetheless foresaw a space-based arms race. The Bush administration finally spelled out America's intention to walk out of the non-proliferation treaties in order to pursue its missile program.

Bush and his advisors—specifically Cheney, Rumsfeld, and Powell—are very much in support of the administration's concentrated efforts on a missile defense shield program that would subsidize the military-industrial complex. In order to avoid international criticism and condemnation for walking out of the treaty, Bush argued that his missile defense shield is directed not against the nuclear powers of the world, but certain rogue states or, far worse, transnational groups capable of launching missiles against American soil or interests abroad.

Hence, both issues seemed to converge into one coherent strategy to fight the new war against an asymmetric enemy. But aside from America's obsession with bin Laden, who else is really targeted here? Mafias and drug traffickers, for instance, have done nothing of this sort, and why should they do it now? It is certainly not good for business. Moreover, unless America intends to bomb one of those so-called rogue states, why would any of their leaders send a missile against the United States, knowing the punishment could be something like that faced by Libya or Iraq over the last several years?

More questions search for answers. To what extent has America invented an enemy, including its own ex-ally bin Laden? And beyond those who carried out the attacks in New York and Washington, how threatening is this enemy to America? Why does that differ from the terrorism that the Arab nations and certain European countries, like France and the United Kingdom, have faced over the last two decades? Is it the sheer quantitative difference in civilian deaths, or is it something qualitatively different? American experts attempt to establish answers, but their answers are insufficient to justify qualifying this as another war following in the steps of nuclear or conventional (i.e., symmetric) warfare and conflict.

Defining asymmetry

Asymmetry must be distinguished from di-symmetry, a quantitative difference in power and firepower, or force. According to the new American thinking, asymmetry underlines the qualitative difference in means, values, and style of the new enemy. In fact, asymmetry can be dialectically understood as the eventual result of di-symmetry. In other words, once a power like America insists on exclusive superiority and hegemony in world affairs, as well as in conventional warfare, its disadvantaged enemies and victims resort to unconventional or asymmetrical means to fight it—avoiding its strengths and concentrating on its vulnerabilities.

The asymmetric enemy is not the typical state-controlled military that fights on an established battlefield. The new enemy, the Pentagon concluded, "does not fight fair." It avoids its enemy's strengths and attacks its weaknesses with neither mercy nor hesitation. It fights clandestinely against specific vulnerable targets or in crowded downtown areas using all of the deadly means at its disposal. American strategic experts contend that, among other approaches, the asymmetric enemy uses means combining a range of theologies and ideologies with the most advanced technologies.

The new asymmetric enemy thinks strategically and in the context of the new global world. Its use of communication, transportation, and information is characteristic of the means at its disposal. Future adversaries may be inclined to use "psychological terror," utilizing the influence of the international media and the Internet in information warfare tactics. Meanwhile, the "hands-on" use of force—involving people committed to die using knives, fishing boats, home-made explosives, and civilian planes rather than fighter jets and advanced weaponry—are seen as an effective means of fighting an asymmetric war. This makes it ever harder to rationally calculate or estimate and, hence, tougher to confront, prevent, and deter.

Even though the enemy may be based within a state, it cannot be categorically accounted for and numbered. It has no permanent address, and its network is widely separated. In a way, it is a creature of globalization. Just as multinational corporations, media gurus, and Internet giants are international, so an asymmetric enemy takes the world for both his address and his area of operations. The suicide bombers in New York and Washington for example, lived in different places, used different addresses, and carried a variety of passports.

In fact, like McDonald's, CNN, and AOL, asymmetric opponents can be international drug dealers, Mafias, and a variety of terrorist networks operating throughout the world. Their common strengths and interests lie in weakening states' sovereignties and disrupting strong international market forces. All utilize the gray areas in a globalized world lacking an adequate legal structure, thus ensuring maximum profits and avoiding legal accountability stemming from constitutional or democratic legitimacy. In fact, they are the new creatures of the neo-liberal version of globalization.

Worldwide institutions like the UN, a sort of international legislative parliament, and the UN Security Council, fulfilling the role of international quasi-government, are all state-based. The new forces of globalization are less accountable to states or their joint institutions than are states themselves, leaving much room in which to maneuver. It is that unruly and unregulated gray area of globalization that multinational advocates claim is responsible for the growth of regional and international crime syndicates, drug trafficking, terrorism, etc. These enemies have always existed, but today they are actors in a globalized world.

In a way, the asymmetric enemy is the other side of the same global process that produces cross-border economies. That is why the image of bin Laden in the American media qualifies him not only as a "political Islamist" who is limited to a particular society, but rather, like Hassan Turabi's Islamic movement that once stood as a dangerous regional threat to America, a new brand of cosmopolitan Islam. To the American mind, they are bent on confronting and weakening Western hegemony or, more dramatically, bringing down America.

In fact, when one adds up all these characteristics of an asymmetric enemy, one comes to the conclusion that those strategists building the new model were thinking of, or "profiling," none other than *their* Osama bin Laden *per se*. Even if bin Laden did not really exist, he has certainly been alive and kicking in the minds of the new age strategists in America. As everyone knows, he was groomed by the CIA in the 1980s only to be doomed by America in the 1990s. In the last eight years, according to the American chronology, bin Laden and his associates concentrated their attacks on American targets outside the United States. Military bases in Saudi Arabia, embassies in Africa, a U.S. Navy Frigate in the Indian ocean, New York's World Trade Center, and the Pentagon have been among their recent attacks according to the CIA.

Should the asymmetric enemy be distinguished from state systems and their intelligence networks? Is it really possible to manage a new movement of *"violence internationale"* without state support within a designated geographical entity? It is not clear how this new enemy could be almost *"virtual"* in its operations and activities. To say that the new enemy is ideology-based is inadequate. Ideologues still require physical land for logistical purposes and as a platform from which to act. This new enemy cannot long remain entirely camouflaged while continuing to function.

Other forms of asymmetry present themselves in America's new thinking, as evidenced in rogue or "failed states." The latter, like in the 1992-93 Somalia intervention, was a hard lesson for the United States. It was in the course of this intervention that America had one of its first experiences of the new asymmetric conflict. In October 1993, Aideed attacked U.S. troops, killing 17 American soldiers. The sight of dead American soldiers dragged through the streets of the capital by armed militias convinced the Clinton administration that it could not manage, let alone win, a war against tribal militias that do not subscribe to the rules of fighting fair, and that cannot be held accountable to international conventions. A similar experience in Lebanon was a painful lesson for the American military when its Marine barracks were targeted, killing about 200 soldiers and leading to the withdrawal of U.S. forces.

Panama was also, to a certain extent, an asymmetric war, even though this was the largest American military operation since Vietnam. It was ostensibly intended to recapture Manuel Antonio Noriega and in that it succeeded, but this was not the end of it. America's appetite for this sort of operation—operations that would later target figures such as Iraq's Saddam Hussein and Serbian leaders Slobodan Milosevic and Radovan Karadzic—was growing in the post-Cold War era. In fact, those operations are no different from so many previous operations against South American or Middle Eastern leaders in decades past. So what is really new?

The answer lies beyond the asymmetric enemy and may be found in the asymmetric solution, like the ability to deploy a wide range of preventive measures in response to perceived threats, and the use of unorthodox means that were not possible or legitimate before 11 September to deter new enemies. Less than a week after the 11 September bombings, the U.S. Congress lifted the ban on assassinating foreign leaders. An increased level of American violence is now possible.

Combating the asymmetric enemy: Learning from Israel

Combating the asymmetric enemy has centered on the military's need for more mobile, more precise, and more intelligent hardware. This includes new weaponry with superior precision and maximum deadliness. American strategists advised that intelligence services be reinforced not only with sophisticated software reconnaissance and satellite spying, but also with human intelligence. Police work, including racial profiling, was also recommended. Spying, in their view, should be directed at a host of potential sources of support for the new enemy, including various NGOs, charitable organizations, expatriate communities, Internet sites, etc. Moreover, the long sought-after and expensive missile defense shield is now within the realm of possibility. After all, you never know what the asymmetric devil is planning for the next attack.

Since the bombings, the U.S. Congress has moved to give the president new powers in this new war. The Senate voted 98-0 and the U.S. House of Representatives approved the authorization by a 420-1 vote in favor. An absolute majority has also authorized $40 billion for the president.

This is the same president who will wage a "crusade," or *"jihad,"* against the "evil doers," capturing the perpetrators "dead or alive" as he "leads the world to victory." Echoing the president's bullying language, U.S. Republican Senator Rick Santorum warned, "This is not a time to bring people to justice, this is a time to wage war" (the lone dissenter, U.S. Representative Barbara Lee, insisted that "military action will not prevent further acts of international terrorism against the United States").

In real terms, most of the material produced about asymmetry focused on America and, since the second *intifada,* on Israel. America has long been working with its ally Israel on the Arrow anti-ballistic missile and other programs within the logic of asymmetric warfare. Presumably, Israel's fighting style and capacity—especially in the West Bank, Gaza, and in Lebanon—seemed to be an area of interest for American experts who detected asymmetry in Israel's wars.

Under the headline "How to Fight an Asymmetric War," General Wesley Clark explained that the Palestinians inside Israel (someone needs to remind Clark that the West Bank and Gaza are not Israel) learned to resist using non-lethal forces like rocks and clubs. It was a tactic aimed at exploiting world sensitivities by forcing Israeli security forces to overreact. Occasionally these tactics were supplemented by armed men concealed among the rock-throwers or by terror bombings. This was the *intifada.* Responding with fighter planes, tanks, and artillery was impossible, while responding with troops on the ground risked casualties. No society is more reluctant than Israel to accept losses, so Israel developed new equipment, new forces, and new tactics. To secure its borders, Israel deployed more heavily armored tanks and troop-carrying vehicles. Apache helicopters, unmanned aerial vehicles, and very long-range optics were procured. To protect itself internally, Israel issued its infantrymen plastic bullets and other riot control gear. Special security forces were organized to help relieve the conventional Israeli units of responsibility for keeping order inside Israel (cf. *Time,* 23 October 2000).

Clark's admiration for Israel's military skills is a scary proposition. Not only has Israel killed over 600 people, injured thousands more, and assassinated thirteen Palestinian citizens demonstrating in solidarity with their brethren under occupation, but Israeli use of force forfeited its logic when it failed to deter the Palestinians, especially in the absence of an Israeli political or diplomatic option.

Anthony Cordesman, a prominent defense analyst at the Center for Strategic and International Studies (CSIS), also speaks of Israel's asymmetric conflict with great admiration and presumed realism. Earlier, Cordesman suggested that in order to achieve peace, the Palestinian Authority (PA) must suppress Palestinians and curb democratic freedoms to attain stability. He suggested that there were two options facing the Palestinians: either "peace with violence" or war. But since the *intifada* continued and grew to encompass more severe means, Cordesman described a situation where Israel would do the dirty work for the PA, and against it, which he referred to as asymmetric warfare. This meant that social control, assassinations, crippling the economy, and other measures were used to defeat the *intifada*.

There is certainly no real comparison between Palestinian resistance to the occupation of Palestine and the attacks in New York and Washington. Israeli Prime Minister Ariel Sharon's comparison between bin Laden and Yasser Arafat fell on deaf ears everywhere except in America. Nonetheless, Israelis feel vindicated in their own use of force in a confrontation with an asymmetric enemy, the *intifada of Tanzim* as the Israelis like to call Palestinian popular resistance to occupation. When one hears Bush nowadays, it becomes clear that America's strategy is heading towards asymmetric warfare along the lines of the Israeli model even though Israel's strategy has failed in Palestine.

More importantly, it is clear that the scourge of the new asymmetric threat is the weakening of states and the contraction of their role in the international arena. Perhaps it is time to strengthen the state's role in a globalized world, at least as a means of regulating the gray area where these threats seem to grow unchecked.

Modernity has been based on the idea of the state. Removing the role of the state can only strengthen the rise of terrorist phenomena in the world. Until a better structure is put in place, multilateral power-sharing initiatives in a multicultural world must be enhanced by universal values, not western hegemony.

The world's gray areas, created by globalization, conflict, and impoverishment, are not only dangerous terrain for fighting an asymmetric war, but they also produce and support the new asymmetric international threat. Strengthening the will of the people in failed and undemocratic states could reduce the maneuvering space for terrorists, drug traffickers, and arms merchants, and for cooperation among them. While fighting its "war on drugs," the United States subsidized Colombian generals who only aggravated drug smuggling and production. The Bush administration reportedly granted Afghanistan's Taliban a subsidy of $43 million only a few months ago. And you know where that leads us. It is time that support for public institutions and intensive development take the place of military subsidies.

The New York bombings will not change the world. Asymmetry is simply another sign of a changing world. Attempting to comprehend the new world we live in is far more necessary than extra intelligence and policing, already proposed as the long-term American strategy against an asymmetric enemy.

Washington might exploit the tragedy in New York to advance its strategic goals in the Middle East and in the wider Muslim world, to reinforce its presence in the Gulf region, and to use new forms of security-related intervention to guarantee its international interests, multinational corporations, and new markets. It is another attempt at "shaping the world," but with more coercion.

The Israelization of America

This is the most dangerous thing that could ever happen to this world, if America becomes Israelized. Not the lobby that influences decisions, but the kind of unilateral conservatism that has been augmented in the United States over the last two decades by policies that adopt Israeli ways of thinking; where the whole world is the enemy, where no one likes us, where we are on our own. Or as Thomas Friedman put it, we have to fight it all on our own.

We can afford an Israel that will walk out of Kyoto. We cannot afford an America that will walk out of Kyoto. We can afford an Israel that will walk out of Durban. We cannot afford an America that will walk out of Durban. We can afford an Israel that will walk out of the ABM treaty. We cannot afford an America that will walk out of the ABM treaty. We can afford an Israel that does not sign onto the Non-Proliferation Treaty. We cannot afford an America that will walk out on the Non-Proliferation Treaty. The same is true with the International Court of Justice, biochemical agreements, and so on. We cannot afford to have an America that will walk out on the world the way Israel is able to.

We can still have a safe world with Israel doing what it is doing, because there is America. Israel can do certain things, but then there is America and there is an American ceiling to everything in the Middle East. With no America to constrain Israel, or to constrain an Israelized America, there will be only disaster. It will be a disaster if America responds to the challenges facing the world today as Israel responds to the Middle East, as Israel responds in the West Bank.

America cannot afford to continue moving B-52 bombers from Missouri to Afghanistan. Israel can move its F-16 bombers a few kilometers from Tel Aviv to Ramallah, but how far can America move its bombers? Would it solve a problem?

America has so far responded in the usual way. It made alliances with Pakistan, Turkey, and Uzbekistan—three non-Arab Muslim nations—giving Pakistan $1 billion, Turkey $19 billion, and Uzbekistan is waiting for $6 or $7 billion. Suddenly those human rights violating, non-democratic nations such as Uzbekistan, Pakistan, and Turkey, have become the new American allies in the war on terrorism.

Why? Because the Arabs are hesitant. Because of the question of Palestine. Because they signed on in the Gulf War. They thought they could go along with America to do whatever had to be done in Kuwait, because America is later going to work with them on the question in the West Bank and Gaza. It did not work. Ten years later, nothing worked.

Now the Arabs are hesitant, so America went to the non-Arab Muslim nations. It is going to be disastrous. Why? Because with those kinds of partners, you are not going to fight terrorism, just as you could not fight Israeli terrorism with South African apartheid, or with Iran's Shah, or with Turkey. It is the same kind of model again.

The bin Ladens of the Middle East have opened the door for further escalation and insecurity, and deeper American intervention. One wonders if the same process witnessed during and after the Gulf War will repeat itself on a larger, more long-term scale? Shaping the Middle East with technology, especially military technology is wishful thinking. Asymmetry could not be confronted with force, and it is not possible to shape the region's societies through technology. Technology without a political project for the region has proved an inferior opponent to culture, identity, and nationalism.

Once the dust settles in New York, the West Bank, and Afghanistan, we will confirm that fighting terrorism is more than just a military and intelligence issue. Like malaria, it requires more than slapping a few annoying mosquitoes. It requires a vaccination program and draining the swamps of misery that sustain it. In fact, those who ridiculed the International Conference against Racism in Durban only a week before the tragedy in New York are advised to look again. It is by addressing the grievances of isolated, repressed, and excluded people, that we can diminish the terrorists' sources of recruits and sympathy. Di-symmetry is best addressed by correcting the inequality and exclusion of entire populations. Using more violence can only lead to yet more violence.

Palestinian author and journalist Marwan Bishara is currently a research  *fellow at the Paris-based Le Centre Indisciplinaire de Recherches sur la Paix et d'etudes Strategiques (CIPRES), where he recently completed a study on the transformation of Israeli society. An Israeli citizen of Nazareth, he is currently a lecturer at the American University in Paris, and he writes for a variety of newspapers, including Le Monde Diplomatique, the International Herald Tribune, and Al Hayat. He has published numerous books, most recently* Palestine/Israel: Peace or Apartheid.

International and Grassroots Initiatives

Alexandros Karides
Program Officer, World Council of Churches

Phyllis Bennis
Fellow, Institute for Policy Studies

Kumi Naidoo
Secretary General and CEO
Civicus World Alliance for Citizen Participation

Barbara Lubin
Executive Director, Middle East Children's Alliance

Gila Svirsky
Co-Founder, Coalition of Women for a Just Peace

The International Ecumenical Response
To the Palestinian-Israeli Conflict

by Alexandros Karides

The World Council of Churches (WCC) is a fellowship of 342 churches in over 110 countries, and from virtually every Christian tradition. The Roman Catholic Church is not a member, but works cooperatively with the WCC.

The Council has been deeply involved in efforts for peace in the Holy Land since 1948. It has repeatedly called for a comprehensive and just peace agreement that will assure the rights, well-being, and security of Israel and the Palestinian people. It has also been committed to dialogue among Christians, Jews, and Muslims to promote tolerance and harmony. While welcoming the Oslo peace process and recognizing that churches continue to stress international law and UN resolutions as a basis for peace, the WCC has been trying to mobilize and coordinate the international ecumenical response to the Palestinian-Israeli conflict since the beginning of the second *intifada*.

Since 1995, the WCC has placed particular focus on Jerusalem's place in the final negotiations and has called for it to be recognized as a shared city for three faiths and two peoples. With the outbreak of the second *intifada,* the Council has responded within the context of an absence of peace negotiations, escalating violence, and intensified human rights violations. Their role has been to provide member churches with deeper analysis and policy tools, to lobby the UN, to provide an international arena for the local churches, and to encourage churches to undertake their own initiatives at the national and regional levels.

Immediately after the *intifada* began, the patriarchs and heads of the Christian communities in Jerusalem denounced the aggression within the sanctuary of a holy place in Jerusalem, and affirmed their solidarity with the Palestinian people—Muslims and Christians alike—in defending the fundamental right to worship and prayer in Jerusalem. They went on to call for the implementation of all relevant UN resolutions in order to secure a comprehensive, just, and lasting peace.

Subsequently, the WCC released an appeal stating that as long as a people remains a subject of injustice, they will continue to be a constant source of fear and insecurity for their neighbor. The Council believes that it is the right, as much as the duty, of an occupied people to struggle against injustice in order to gain their freedom, although it also believes, to quote the appeal to churches, "that non-violent struggle remains stronger and more efficient."

The Council later issued an appeal requesting protection for local members to assist in reestablishing mutual trust and security between Israelis and Palestinians. More recently, following Israeli military incursions in the Palestinian territories, the Jerusalem churches described a dramatic situation of siege and targeted killings and called on world church leaders and the international community to urgently ask the Israeli government to end an intolerable situation.

After the second *intifada* began, WCC member churches submitted written and oral statements to the Fifth Special Session of the UN Commission on Human Rights asking that the UN respond to resolution 1322 by contributing, within its mandate, to a speedy and objective inquiry into the tragic events. In October the Council actively participated in a special session with the head and representatives of the local churches in Jerusalem, and welcomed its resolution establishing the Human Rights Inquiry Commission.

In December, the WCC general secretary sent a letter to the local churches, noting that a just peace and an end to the vicious cycle of violence is more than an urgent political necessity, and that a cease-fire—desirable as that may be—is clearly not enough. The shared goal must be true peace, a peace built on the foundations of justice.

The WCC's central committee, meeting in Germany later in the year, unanimously declared that it was deeply disturbed by a pattern of discrimination, routine humiliation, segregation, and exclusion restricting Palestinian freedom of movement. This includes access to holy sites, Israel's disproportionate use of military force, and the cantonization of the Occupied Territories separating Palestinian lands—a pattern reminiscent of policies the WCC had condemned in the past. In an historic vote, the Council urged its member churches to increase their efforts to condemn injustice and all forms of discrimination, to end Israeli occupation, and to pray for and promote a comprehensive and just peace in the Middle East.

The Council asked the fifty-seventh session of the UN Commission on Human Rights to endorse the recommendations of the High Commission for Human Rights and the Human Rights Inquiry Commission as expressed in their statements. These statements included the establishment of an adequate and effective international presence to ensure that Palestinians' human rights are fully protected.

Along with letters, statements, advocacy initiatives, and representing the churches at governmental and international forums, the Council also provides information regarding the situation on the ground and initiatives taking place throughout the world, advising members on how those initiatives can be adapted for other countries.

Parallel to its collective work, the WCC has followed and highlighted a comprehensive series of individual actions by its member churches and ecumenical partners. This has included pastoral letters to the churches, public statements, letters to governments and heads of state, statements to the UN, humanitarian assistance, appeals and advocacy alerts, and solidarity visits to the region. While this has come mainly from churches in North America and Western Europe, it has included Christian world communions, as well as regional, national, and other ecumenical organizations.

A good example of this work can be seen in the American churches, the first to take a delegation to the region in December 2000 as a sign of their solidarity and support. Following the visit, they issued a statement dealing strongly with the use of disproportionate force, creation of "facts on the ground," international protection, and U.S. arm sales and aid to Israel. That statement was followed by a meeting between a high level delegation and U.S. Secretary of State Colin Powell, and letters to the Israeli and Palestinian leaderships.

Another American initiative is the monthly nationwide prayer vigil for peace in the Middle East. Coordinated by the Evangelical Lutheran Church of America's Office for Governmental Affairs and the Churches for Middle East Peace, the WCC is helping to internationalize the vigil. Such action not only demonstrates the uniqueness of the churches' role, but also provides useful and effective opportunities for public awareness and advocacy.

The Council played a role in implementing the Central Committee's resolution urging its staff to support churches in the Holy Land supporting local and Israeli grassroots initiatives, and strengthening international ecumenical support for a comprehensive Middle East peace. The WCC general secretary sent a delegation to Jerusalem and called for an international ecumenical consultation in Geneva in August. This was the first of its kind and included participants from Europe, North America, South America, Asia, Africa, and Jerusalem, as well as a representative of the Holy See to the UN in Geneva, the leadership of the Middle East Council of Churches, and Palestinian and Israeli peace activists.

Attendees agreed that statements by churches worldwide were important, but that the time for statements was over. The full delegation report was presented, along with its recommendations supporting those of the Human Rights Inquiry Commission—two of whose members were present at the consultation— and were endorsed by all participants. The delegation called for the WCC to develop a comprehensive program to coordinate advocacy at all levels to support international law, and particularly UN resolutions, as the basis for peace negotiations, and to encourage alternative and moderate voices struggling on both sides to find a common vision for the future.

The churches' and religious communities' specific contributions to peace and reconciliation were emphasized throughout the meeting. Being members and representatives of faith-based communities entails a commitment to a certain moral and ethical stance. The WCC general secretary confirmed the integrity of the rights approach, which we hope will rescue the conflict from becoming totally embroiled in a power struggle.

In September, the WCC executive committee welcomed and endorsed these recommendations, and called for the implementation of five measures by the Council's staff:

- develop a program that will include an international ecumenical presence like the Christian Peacemaker Teams;

- call upon all member churches and partners in the context of the "Decade to Overcome Violence, 2001-2010," to focus their attention on efforts to end the illegal occupation of Palestine;

- call for an international boycott of goods produced in the illegal Israeli settlements in the Occupied Territories;

- call on member churches and Christians to join active non-violent resistance to the destruction of Palestinian homes and forced evictions; and

- join in international prayer vigils to strengthen the chain of solidarity with the Palestinian people.

This may be the first time since the struggle against apartheid that a concerted and action-oriented response such as this has been undertaken. In the first stage, the WCC recently announced the establishment of the Ecumenical Monitoring Presence in Palestine and Israel (EMPPI) which will coordinate church and ecumenical monitoring and observer teams.

Several church-related pilot projects are already underway and will be a part of EMPPI. These include: a campaign coordinated by Dutch development, ecumenical, and peace organizations; a Church of Sweden ecumenical monitoring effort; an observer program developed by Danish ecumenical organizations; and an ecumenical program being developed by the Middle East Forum in the United States churches.

The full scope and coordinating mechanism of EMPPI will be developed with churches and partners over the next several months. It is expected to focus on monitoring human rights violations in sensitive situations like checkpoints, accompanying people in their daily activities such as school, work, or hospitals, observing public actions, and participating in direct non-violent action. It will work with local churches and human rights and peace organizations in the region as required.

The program is a powerful way for churches worldwide to actively display solidarity with their brothers and sisters in Palestine and Israel as they struggle to resist a harsh military occupation non-violently. Moreover, it will provide a foundation for further education and for raising public awareness, as well as an alternative voice in advocacy work. Even within the current international context, responses have been very encouraging, both in affirming the role of the Council in coordinating and providing an umbrella group for the churches, and also in confirming the desperate need for such an initiative.

The churches provide an alternative voice and possess a huge global network that can be mobilized. This is what the WCC has been trying to do, to bring in not only the European and American churches, which have traditionally been involved and have made strong statements and taken strong actions, but also in Asia, Africa, and Latin America.

Alexandros Karides, a political scientist specializing in international relations theory, is a program associate with the international relations team of the WCC. He has been directly involved in the coordination of the ecumenical response to the Palestinian-Israeli conflict, as well as working on the Council's policy on Cyprus and Iraq.

Challenging U.S. Policy
On Israel and Palestine

by Phyllis Bennis

I am going to play Cassandra here. In Greek mythology she was the one who always had the bad news, but Cassandra was not quite the boy who cried wolf because she was right in her doomsday propositions. No one likes to be Cassandra because you always like to be wrong when you predict that things are really quite grim, and that there is not much light ahead, and that the only light at the end of the tunnel is the train rushing up to meet you. But this is a moment when we cannot afford illusions.

Through the past spring and summer, I worked with a group of colleagues trying to craft a new approach to dealing with the question of U.S. policy toward Israel and Palestine. This was an approach rooted in the enormous work that had gone on—mainly over the last two years and most particularly through the last year, the year of the second *intifada*—that had engendered enormous energy, particularly within the Arab-American community and among young Palestinians. These were third generation Palestinians growing up in exile. They are the counterparts of those young people growing up in Dheishe and in the other refugee camps of the West Bank, Gaza, Jordan, Syria, Lebanon, and elsewhere. They have done extraordinary work in this country, mobilizing with new energy on college campuses the first big demonstration on the question of the right of return.

Suddenly the issue of return was very much on top of the agenda and that was a very new development. Within the community, that was a huge accomplishment. The same was true for the discussions that began to emerge on college campuses about the need for one state. The discussion centered on the vision beyond a two-state solution where a non-viable state-let would be created in name only and would have no real significance. It went on to say that we need one state for everyone in the region to live together in peace as individuals, not a state based on ethnicity, religion, etc. This was in a certain way a return to an older language that many of us had used in the past, a democratic, secular state in all of Israel and Palestine.

But the Cassandra in me says that virtually none of that extraordinary level of mobilization over those two years has mattered. It matters within the community. It matters on the college campuses. But it does not matter when it comes to engaging with power, when it comes to changing policy. It was in that context that a group of us looked at our work here in this country, and asked: "what has to happen here?"

We are dealing with a reality that we do not control. We are dealing with the reality of a Palestinian national movement which is itself in crisis, with a Palestinian leadership that has lost its vision—perhaps it never had that vision and certainly does not now—for what the work in the international arena should look like. The notion that we could build on the legacy of the African National Congress (ANC) struggle against apartheid, in my view, was wrong. The ANC worked for years to craft a vision for an African national movement based on the notion of a non-racial South Africa. They had a strategy not just within South Africa—a military strategy, a political strategy, a diplomatic strategy, and a mass mobilization strategy—but they had the same strategy for their international supporters.

The idea of crafting an anti-apartheid movement in this country that was rooted in trying to end the investment—the divestment movement that began on college campuses and spread to the unions and throughout civil society in this country—did not happen just because there were some creative activists here. That happened because the ANC called for it as a part of their strategy for building a national movement.

What we have to face is that the Palestine Liberation Organization (PLO) is not the ANC. Palestine is not South Africa and outside of small enclaves of progressive thinking, it does not resonate with the American people to talk about the apartheid nature of Israel. It is accurate, but accuracy, frankly, is not worth very much these days if you cannot reach people where they are.

That is why we began thinking we had to change. The work that is being done on the college campuses is crucial. The work that is being done in the Arab-American community is crucial. The mobilization among Palestinians to recapture the urgency of return is crucial. But none of those are what we as Americans, focused on U.S. foreign policy, can think is going to engage in a serious way with a serious result, a change in policy.

This is what we were talking about all through the spring and summer. We wrote papers and we talked about what it would look like to craft a new initiative based on all of this. We had the meeting scheduled for 15 September in New York, and then we had the events of 11 September. Of course the meeting got cancelled, as so much was. Suddenly it was, as in the famous Yeats quote, "All changed, changed utterly." But then Yeats went on to say, "and a terrible beauty was born." What was born here when all changed was not a terrible beauty, it was a terrible terror, and it changed almost everything.

But it did not change the fundamental nature of the Israeli occupation as the framework for looking at policy changes needed in the Middle East. It did change a lot about how we have to address those policies, and it increased the urgency of dealing with those policies. This is an intersection between the crisis of 11 September and the ongoing crisis of the Israeli occupation of Palestine and the U.S. support that makes that occupation possible.

There are some significant changes that we have to look at very seriously. Right now the Bush administration is polling higher than perhaps any administration in history. Other forces in government that might occasionally act as checks and balances, particularly Congress, are afraid. In a climate of such strong support for the Bush administration, no one in Congress wants to go out on a limb and say no. That was why we had the lone, brave Barbara Lee providing the only voice willing to challenge the initial call to war as the only possible response to the crime against humanity committed on 11 September.

But we also have some other changes. We have Bush and his surrogate, Tony Blair, the latest spokesman for the U.S. administration, talking not only about

Palestinian statehood—which they have referred to before, albeit a little bit distantly—but they are now using the very interesting word "viable." They are proposing that we not only need a Palestinian state, we need a "viable Palestinian state." That is a significant change. They all—Powell, Bush, and Blair—started using it on the same day, and suddenly we are all concerned with viability.

That is a good thing. We like viability. The battle is going to be a battle of definition: what is it that makes a state viable? It is going to be talked about in the context of the plan—the speech we keep hearing about that Colin Powell has in his pocket, just ready to pull out—and it is going to talk a lot about numbers. This is a proposal that 96 percent, or 94 percent, or 99 percent of the land of the West Bank is going to be returned to the Palestinians.

What they are not going to say is that we are not talking about a little chunk of land somewhere on a border adjustment. We are talking about one or three or five percent of the land that makes up the grid of settlement roads, settlement blocks, bridges, and all of the areas that divide the West Bank into non-contiguous, non-viable cantons. They are going to say this is viable because it is 97 percent.

Saying viable is right, but what does viable mean? Viable means obeying international law and withdrawing from all Occupied Territories. You can argue all you want about whether resolution 242 says "territories" or "the territories," but international law as a whole is quite unequivocal, unlike the difference between the French and English translations of the resolution. International law says that territories taken by force cannot be kept. It happens in wartime, but after the war, it is returned. That is the starting point.

The question of occupation has to remain the central focus. The way we talk about it has to resonate with Americans. To change public opinion, people have to be de-educated from what they think they know. Although the questions are becoming somewhat more sophisticated, this is starting from a really low standard. People think they know an awful lot about the Middle East crisis, in a way that they do not imagine that they know very much about Afghanistan, just as they did not imagine that they knew very much about Rwanda, or about Bosnia, and certainly not about Somalia. But people think they do know a lot about Israel/Palestine, and what they know is "Israelis are like us." Israel is a democracy, and Palestinians are sort of terrorists and, at best, are just out shooting.

That is pretty much what people know.

We have to change that before we can re-educate an entire population to a new way of thinking, and that is not easy. Right now things are changing. The use of the term "viability" creates new possibilities. The fact that Israel is suddenly a potential impediment to this coalition is a moment of opportunity. It is a very tricky one. We have to be very clear as we use that opening that we do not, by our actions or our words, give credence to any legitimacy of an illegitimate war the United States is carrying out in Afghanistan.

If the war is expanded to Iraq, and perhaps other countries later, there will be an enormous outcry. It is no more acceptable to bomb Afghan children than it will be to bomb Iraqi children. We have to be very, very careful that when we deal with the question of civilian consequences, we not wait until they are hitting Iraq, or until they are hitting Iraq again, because they are still hitting Iraq. That has not stopped.

Israel, in this situation, is a potential problem for the United States and it is being discussed differently. We have to be careful not to fall into an anti-Semitic, anti-Jewish approach that will be popular. We are already seeing bits and pieces of that, that it is not only Israel that is a problem, but it is sort of "those Jews" that are problems. We also have to be very careful not to fall into the trap of legitimizing this coalition and saying we need to cut military aid to Israel in order to strengthen the coalition. We do not want this coalition to be stronger to carry out a war. We want a coalition of the world in which the United States is one part, not the dominant part.

Others have raised the point that there are differences in U.S. foreign policy circles, that there are these forces around Colin Powell who would agree with everything we say. Colin Powell differs significantly from the Wolfowitz cabal. But it is the difference between the pragmatism that says you are best served by imposing your will through creating or imposing, false or not, a coalition—and demanding that other countries join it—versus those who say we do not need any such decorations. They believe we should just go in and bomb them, and the other countries will have little choice but to come on board.

It is a problem that the United States thinks it can impose its will, regardless of the way it does so. Yes, if it is going to impose its will, it is preferable that they do it without bombing, but that is not the only choice. The other choice is human rights and international law, and that is a language that American people understand, even if our policymakers do not. Polls show that, before Bush's increase after 11 September, the UN had higher ratings among the American people than any agency of the American government: higher than the White House, higher than Congress, higher than the CIA, higher than the Supreme Court, higher than everybody except the Post Office.

But the fact that Congress acts as if they were representing our interests in functioning as an anti-UN bloc does not make it an accurate reflection of American public opinion. The problem has been us, the people who are committed to these issues. We have not mobilized that public opinion. It is very wide, but very thin. We have never demanded of people that they make real their commitment to the UN. We have never organized successfully the kind of public campaign that would force Congress to stop this nonsense of withholding dues.

Americans do understand those kinds of things. They understand what it means to be a deadbeat country. If you get outside of the beltway, you see that among people. That is where we have to start. We talk about occupation as a massive violation of human rights. People mostly know what that means. They have a narrow view of human rights—most people in this country understand civil and political rights, although they do not necessarily understand economic and social rights, but that struggle is underway and people are open to that. But it is not going to be easy, and we can have no illusions.

By disseminating information on what is happening, we can mobilize Americans. There are two things the American people need to know:

1.　We are supporting occupation and it is violating human rights, and

2.　U.S. military aid is sending helicopter gun-ships that are being used against civilians, against children, against refugee camps, and that is not a good thing. It violates laws: it violates U.S. laws, it violates international laws. But the bottom line is that it is wrong, and that is something people can understand.

Calling for an end to aid to Israel is a non-starter. We have tried it before and we failed. But focusing on military aid, maybe even focusing on one aspect of military aid, like these Apache helicopter gun-ships gives us something very solid. When people say, "why do they hate us?" you say, "because after the bombings they go and pick up the shell-casings that say 'Made in the U.S.A.' That's why they hate us." It is not for what we are, it is for what we—our government, with our tax money, in our name—is doing to them. It is not because we have democracy and they do not want democracy. It is because we are supporting governments and policies that are denying them democracy. It is much simpler in a certain way than it looks when we read the papers.

We have a very important opening while the American-Israeli alliance is being questioned. It is being questioned for horrific reasons. It is being questioned by people who do not question the strategic, Cold War-driven imperatives that have always driven it, but for tactical reasons they are willing to say things today that they were never willing to say before 11 September. When that opens up in official circles it gives us a moment's breather as well, a moment's opening. It is not going to last very long. The moment that Colin Powell gives the speech, and is roundly condemned as turning against Israel and becoming an advocate for Arab interests, that is going to become the new outside parameter in the debate on what is acceptable. Anything beyond that is going to be unacceptable.

We have this moment, and not much more, and we have to take advantage of it. We need to be doing all the basic things that we always think we can skip— we can skip stages, we can skip steps, and can somehow still have a movement, like the anti-apartheid movement. Well, that is the Cassandra in me. There are no stages that can be skipped. You send a letter to the newspaper, but it is not printed. The fifty-first letter gets printed, but you cannot skip to 51. You have to write 50 that will be rejected first. You have to call the radio talk shows fifteen times before you get in. But you cannot skip to sixteen without doing the first fifteen.

We have to go back to the basics. That means going out, not talking about what our next conference will be and who our next speakers will be, although the idea of a speaking tour for some folks is not necessarily a bad idea. We do not need to ask people to come to us, but we must go to them. We have go to the Parent-Teacher Associations (PTA) at our kids' schools. We have to go to the Rotary Club and the Lion's Club and the League of Women Voters. Those organizations, along with the churches, make up civil society in this country. The churches are the largest mobilizing element in this society. Most of the established Christian churches have passed great resolutions on Israeli occupation, on Iraqi sanctions, on all kinds of things. But the degree to which they do or do not filter down to the local congregations is very uneven.

We have to take some responsibility for that, starting with where we are in our own workplaces, our own churches, our own mosques, our own synagogues, our own everything. We have to take the issue to where the people are. We can no longer sit back and say we are up against the American Israel Public Affairs Committee (AIPAC) and we cannot compete with that. We have responsibilities, and the responsibility now is to go out and say that this is a new world since 11 September, and people are asking new questions. It is right to ask those questions, and we have some answers. We have to end the occupation, and we have to do it based on human rights and international law.

Phyllis Bennis, a Middle East affairs analyst for over 20 years, is currently a fellow of the Institute for Policy Studies in Washington, DC where she is responsible for UN and Middle East programs. She is also a fellow of the Transnational Institute and has appeared many times on television and radio. She is the author of numerous publications, and her most recent book is entitled, Calling the Shots: How Washington Dominates Today's UN.s

Anti-Apartheid:
The South African Experience

by Kumi Naidoo

Issues and reflections from the struggle in South Africa might be of value in terms of how to contemplate the current challenges in the Palestinian-Israeli conflict. During the struggle for liberation in South Africa, much of what one heard activists reflect on—the control of the media, false removals, etc.—was very similar.

The African National Congress (ANC), led by Nelson Mandela, spoke about four pillars of struggle. Mass mobilization, understood as being a very vital component of the struggle, tried to energize as many citizens, both black and white across the racial divide, to become active agents in opposing the regime's policies. Importantly, part of the struggle of mass mobilization includes understanding that people are at different levels of understanding. One has to look at different ways to connect with people based on their realities. For example, Black Sash in South Africa was an organization made up predominantly of white women who supported the struggle against apartheid, but there were also much more militant youth organizations.

The second, and very critical, pillar was international solidarity. In the context of South Africa, it would have been completely naïve not to understand how global power and politics determined how the political conflict would be resolved.

Of course that was also during the cold war, which had a complexity of its own. A year before Mandela was released from prison most U.S. policymakers still regarded him as a full-fledged terrorist. The struggle to shift international public opinion in the struggle in South Africa was not dissimilar from the struggle currently facing the Palestinians.

The third pillar was the political underground, and this consisted of a resistance movement that pushed the banned political organizations. The ANC was banned and contact with it was limited. One man went to prison for five years because his bed sheet was in the colors of the ANC flag, and a mineworker who wrote "Free Mandela" on his cup ended up in prison for three years. Underground legal work was undertaken to legitimize banned organizations.

The fourth element was called armed struggle, but was actually a very limited attempt at armed propaganda. It was never taken very seriously in terms of a military threat posed by the liberation movement.

The way in which these elements articulated with one another was challenging. International solidarity, which would be a major shifting point in the struggle for liberation, was dependent on what sort of message was transmitted from the various components of the struggle, particularly mass mobilization. There was a period in which the apartheid state became more and more violent—particularly as they engaged in intensive military action, and many young children were killed or sent to prison—and South Africans' anger increased which brought out a great deal of militancy.

Harsh actions were taken against people who collaborated with the apartheid regime, and these were often black people. When those images were portrayed on international television, the impact on the advances in international public opinion were constantly being pushed back. Trying to synchronize those different elements proved very difficult. The challenge was to work out where the key emphasis was located at different times. International solidarity certainly was not always the most important element, but just before the transition, in the final moments before the apartheid regime fell, international solidarity became one of the most important things.

The question is often raised, "who was the main instrument of change in South Africa? Was it Nelson Mandela, or was it F.W. de Klerk, the last apartheid prime minister?" It was neither of them. It was Edward Shevardnadze.

Shevardnadze was, at that time, the Soviet foreign minister. Looking at how the political forces played out, how economic interests played in, how the cold war dialogue was unfolding, a deal done far away from our shores actually had a decisive effect.

One of the messages taken away from the World Conference against Racism in Durban was that we are living in a world of growing polarization, and of growing ignorance. This is occurring notwithstanding the media explosion, the quality of analysis, the quality of information made available to citizens around the world, and the ability to shift people's consciousness in such a powerful way.

One of the interesting things in Durban was that it was the first and biggest act of solidarity with what was happening to the Palestinian people. That is not to say that there have not been other moments when South Africans stopped to act in solidarity. For instance, in 1982, after Sabra and Shatila, South African activists took time off from the struggle against apartheid to hold solidarity meetings.

The strategic implications of how one can reach out to people in other parts of the world now are interesting. Many governments, formal governmental institutions, and political leaders have been completely immobilized by the post-11 September global reality. There is a very strong sense of not rocking the boat, not being critical, and so on, but making connections with people with greater freedom to speak their minds is where the opportunities lie.

For example, in all three major cities in South Africa in the past year, Palestinian solidarity committees or campaigns have emerged. Interestingly, these draw not necessarily Muslims, but people from all faiths, including Jewish South Africans. While Israel and apartheid South Africa were united on security, defense, and torture techniques, proportionally the highest number of white South Africans supporting the struggle against apartheid were Jewish, not dissimilar to the demographics of the civil rights movement in the United States.

One of the connections that people are talking about now is the question of land. Because land and occupation are such big issues within the Palestinian conflict, the connection has been made and has led to wider participation in South Africa at theoretical and practical levels.

It is important to recognize that South Africa faced a moment exactly like this, where change seemed to be somewhere, but we always assumed that it would never come in our lifetimes. That, in fact, if it were going to happen, it would happen, optimistically, ten or maybe thirty or forty years later. But a deal was made far away from South Africa, and suddenly it happened.

The most innovative and promising examples of efforts in the Palestinian-Israeli conflict are not coming from governments or government-like institutions, but just as in South Africa, they are coming from individuals through civic institutions.

One of the tragedies of the transition from apartheid to a democratic state was that a lot of people left the non-governmental organization (NGO) community to go into government. It weakened civil society, and created such a dominance for the elected ANC party that the opposition's voice became very weak. In fact, it is jokingly said that so many people left the NGOs to go into government that NGO in South Africa now stands for "next government official."

The relationship between citizens and their future government needs to be considered now. Otherwise, much of what people hold dear will disappear very quickly. For example, the issue of gender equality, which was a core component in the South African struggle, has gone reasonably well, but certainly nowhere near what could have been achieved.

In the last ten years, some have spoken during transitions, particularly massive political transitions, about the Truth and Reconciliation Commission. The Commission was, principally and conceptually, a very good thing. It intentionally sought the truth about what happened during a difficult political conflict, and it hopes to do that in a way that can lead to reconciliation. This is clearly going to challenge whatever happens on this question. A peace based on justice has to be an important part of what truth is told because in the South African context, a violation of human rights was described merely as an individual act of violence committed by a police officer, an army sergeant, or an activist. It wrote all of the citizens out of the equation, so that the only violations were actual direct acts.

It ignored the calculated racial and social engineering, vindictively and systematically planned and carried out, which affected the lives of millions of people. The only victims were those who were killed or tortured, but if you were, as state policy, deprived of a basic education and, as a result, lived a life of intellectual underdevelopment, that was your own problem.

It is interesting that the word democracy does not really come up as consistently and evenly as it used to. It pops up in all sorts of strange and inexplicable ways, but in reality democracy has been defined as the act of casting a vote once every four or five years. The biggest challenge for citizens in any part of the world is to challenge the notions of democracy and governance. The idea that governance is simply what government does must be vigorously opposed. Governance has to be redefined as an ongoing enterprise between citizens and their governments. Winning an election should not be read as a mandate to rule with no reference to the citizenry and their views.

The ongoing challenge is to ensure that the spirit of democracy—the voices, views, opinions, and feelings of ordinary citizens—has public expression and is translated into policy and its implementation. Unless that is achieved, much of the discourse of democracy will lead us to the form of democracy, but not the substance.

Kumi Naidoo is Secretary General and CEO of Civicus World Alliance for Citizen Participation. He was the founding director of the South African NGO Coalition, and served on the task team drafting new NGO legislation. He has worked extensively in adult education and social and economic justice in South Africa. Naidoo holds a doctorate in political science from Oxford University, where he was a Rhodes Scholar.

The Conference against Racism
In Durban, South Africa

by Barbara Lubin

This is the anniversary of the signing of the Balfour Declaration. That was in 1917 and that has had a great effect on all of our lives, not a good effect, but an effect.

Growing up in a very right-wing Zionist home—my father raised money and sent guns to the Irgun—everything in our lives was, "is it good for Israel?" Our family was so tied to Israel and our synagogue that if someone said, "pass the salt," someone else would say, "is it good for Israel?" Actually it was not good for Israel, but I only learned that later.

I was elected to the Board of Education the same week as the massacre in Sabra and Shatila. A group of San Francisco State University (SFSU) students from Palestine and Lebanon came to talk to me and said, "Barbara, you go to El Salvador, you go to Nicaragua, you're involved in the anti-apartheid movement on the campus, and you do not say anything about Israel." And I said, "you know I'm Jewish." They said, "so what?"

I have traveled a long way from there. I remember going to hear people like myself speak and thinking "that woman is the most disgusting person I have ever heard. How could she be saying these things?" Now I usually look out at an audience and think, "I know just what you are thinking. I was there. But I am not there any more."

While I was on the school board, the Mayor of Berkeley and I went to Nicaragua. We forced the city council and the school board to adopt a resolution making Juigalpa in Nicaragua a sister city to Berkeley. We went to El Salvador and created a sister city relationship with San Antonio Los Ranchos and Berkeley. Berkeley has a history of sister city relationships with every cockamamie European country that you can imagine.

We decided it might be a good idea to have a sister city in Palestine, and we chose Jabalia Refugee Camp. Anywhere from 70,000 to 85,000 people live there at one time. It is the most densely populated area on earth, and it is a nightmare for people who are born there, live there, and die there. We lost the next election miserably. In the last two weeks of the campaign, a group of Zionists hired a public relations firm and called every household in Berkeley, asking, "do you know who your sisters in Jabalia are? They want to kill the Jews, push them into the ocean." We only got 27 percent of the vote.

Berkeley has always been in the forefront of progressive political movements and struggles, from Grenada to being leaders in getting our university to divest its holding in South Africa. When it comes to Nicaragua, we are there. When it comes to anywhere in the world, we are there.

I worked with the city council ten years ago and encouraged them to pass a resolution calling for a lifting of the sanctions on the children of Iraq. Middle East Children's Alliance (MECA), for the last fourteen long and gruesome years, has worked in Iraq. We went to Iraq two days before the Gulf War. I had just come from Gaza and I asked every single person I met in the Middle East, "what do you think?" And they said, "the United States will never bomb Iraq." And here we Americans were thinking, "how many countries have said that over the years?"

On our last night there we had dinner with Yasser Arafat at the Palestinian compound in Baghdad, and I asked, "when are you going to leave, my friend?" He said, "don't worry, the United States will never bomb Baghdad." I said, "listen to me. If there is one thing that is sure, the United States will be bombing in two days." We left, but I went back a month later with a photojournalist, George Azar, who photographed everything. What we found there was appalling. People talk today about collateral damage in Afghanistan. George and I saw firsthand, right after that bombing in Iraq, what collateral damage is. It is entire neighborhoods decimated. In one neighborhood in Baghdad, an entire row of apartment buildings was gone, and a little boy and his grandfather were digging through the rubble, looking for their belongings.

In 1987, when the *intifada* began, the same group of young Palestinians from SFSU came to see me and said, "we want you to go to Palestine as guests of the Palestinians." Two weeks later Jeanne Butterfield and myself led a delegation of ten locally-elected officials from the United States, a Catholic priest, and two of us who were Jewish. It was definitely the trip that changed my life. When I came back Howard Levine and I started MECA. MECA has since delivered over $7 million in food and medicine to children in Iraq, in Shatila Refugee Camp in Lebanon, and in Palestine. We have worked in Dheishe Refugee Camp and supported the building and financing of the intercultural center and guesthouse.

Nothing will stop the people of Dheishe and Ib'da. They are very political. The kids are having rallies all the time in support of the children in Iraq, and they are quite remarkable. Our computer center, which we originally built twelve years ago as a dental clinic, was burned down. They rebuilt it, and it was burned down again. It was turned into a computer center, and it was burned down a year ago. It has been rebuilt. We are determined that as many times as it gets burned down, as many times as it gets destroyed, we will rebuild, and rebuild, and rebuild. We have built playgrounds in the West Bank, accessible parks and playgrounds, in al-Bireh, in Nablus, and in Gaza.

As for what has happened in this country since 11 September, we all recognize that this is a tragic and horrible loss of life, but the loss of life in New York, in Washington, and on the airplanes, while it is horrendous, was not surprising. The only surprise was that it took so long to happen.

Ten hours earlier, I had returned from the International Conference against Racism in South Africa. It was quite an experience to return to the United States after marching down the main street in Durban with 50,000 people holding signs saying "End Apartheid in Israel" and "Zionism Equals Racism." There was a general feeling among people from all over the world that Israel has got to stop its tactics, has got to end this occupation. And a recognition that each of us works differently depending on where we live and who we are talking to.

But it is important to talk about, and there is nothing wrong with using words like "apartheid" and "racism" and calling it what it is. College kids in this country are trying to find other language, but if it walks like a duck, and it talks like a duck, it is a duck.

The most horrible thing, the most upsetting thing, that has happened as a result of what took place on 11 September, is people wrapping themselves in the American flag. I find it abhorrent, frightening, and worrisome. If I hear of one more prayer vigil, one more mourning ceremony, one more whatever, I am going to scream.

This is supposed to be a country where we work very hard to have a separation of church and state. Many people come to talks I give and they say, "we want you to come here to the mosque and we want you to understand Islam." I do not need to understand Islam to know that all of us deserve justice. I do not need to understand Christianity to know that I will fight to the death so that you can pray in your churches, mosques, and synagogues. I am a secular person, and I operate in this world as an internationalist. Not because I am Jewish—my Judaism is very private to me—but because I am an internationalist.

If we could learn one thing from what has just taken place, it is instead of the U.S. government pointing its finger outwards, we have to point inside. We have to look at ourselves and ask, "what are our policies that have caused so much anger, hatred, and disgust with our government?"

There is room in this movement for all of us, and that includes the secular people, the people that ally themselves with everyone who identifies as just a person working for justice. This world has become very small, and one thing we have to understand is to forget the flags, forget all of that. We have to be citizens of this world. We have to be *good* citizens of this world. We have to be stewards of our world.

 *Barbara Lubin is the executive director and co-founder of the Middle East Children's Alliance, a non-profit organization dedicated to helping bring peace to the Middle East and ensuring that the rights of children are respected and protected. Ms. Lubin was presented with the Service to Humanity Award by the American Muslims of America, who cited her as a "unique individual with inextinguishable love for her fellow beings, children in particular, and for the capacity to transcend religious boundaries."*

Israeli Peace Activism
And the Politics of the Middle East

by Gila Svirsky

The agenda of an Israeli peace activist is filled with activities. If you have the time and inclination, you can spend every day of the week at one action or another. Looking into my journal at one particularly busy week a few months ago, this is what I saw:

Sunday: Continued work rebuilding demolished home.

Monday: Supreme Court—solidarity with Yinon Hiller [an Israeli conscientious objector to army service].

Tuesday: Demonstration against closure. Got arrested.

Wednesday: Got released. B'Tselem board meeting [non-governmental organization (NGO) on human rights in the territories].

Thursday: Proposal-writing [for funding demonstrations, bail money, etc.].

Friday: Land Day demonstrations [solidarity with Palestinian citizens of Israel].

Saturday: Strategic planning meeting.

And this represents the week of someone who "does peace" in her spare time, not in a paid position.

While the lives of Palestinians in the territories are filled with violence and the threat of violence from the Israeli army, the lives of Israeli peace activists are filled with figuring out how to stop that violence. Unlike our Palestinian neighbors, we Israelis are not usually in jeopardy, though some of us have felt on our bodies various forms of Israeli army anger. Our lives, however, are also entirely circumscribed by the occupation and how to end it: how to persuade the Israeli public and policymakers that ending the occupation is in Israel's best interest; how to convince foreign leaders to intervene constructively in our region; and how to convey to Palestinians not to despair, that they have allies on the other side. To those ends, we spend our days and nights demonstrating, writing articles, lobbying, canvassing, sending letters to the editor, talking to groups, and otherwise trying to get attention and be persuasive.

Many of you have heard that the Peace Now movement has done little in the first year of the current *intifada*. I am glad to report that there are signs they are beginning to revive. Meanwhile, however, other peace movements have been far from passive. As a case in point, there is the Coalition of Women for a Just Peace, which was founded six weeks after this *intifada* broke out. The Coalition brings together the ten Israeli women's peace organizations. Member organizations include:

- Women in Black which has held a powerfully dramatic vigil every single Friday for the past thirteen-and-a-half years in many locations in Israel. Women wear black and stand silently for one hour every week carrying signs bearing a simple message that says it all: "End the Occupation."
- New Profile which is a group of women who work to end the militarization of Israeli society and to support conscientious objectors to army service. The number of conscientious objectors has significantly increased in the past year.
- Bat Shalom which has worked to build a common platform for peace with Palestinian women in a partnership called The Jerusalem Link: A Women's Joint Venture for Peace.
- Machsom Watch, meaning "Checkpoint Watch," which patrols and monitors checkpoints wherever Israeli soldiers block the movement of Palestinians, documenting the brutality and humiliations that take place there daily, and bringing this to the attention of the Israeli public and authorities, as well as international bodies.

While each of these organizations has its own particular objective and strategy, together as a coalition we carry out joint actions that magnify our impact and raise the volume on the message that we broadcast.

And what *is* our message? That we are Israelis, and we believe that peace is viable between our two nations. That the only viable peace must be based on a two-state solution, Israel and Palestine, free and independent, side-by-side, based on the 1967 borders, the Israeli settlers returned to within the borders of Israel, and Jerusalem the shared capital of both states. But hang on, before you nod your head in agreement, we also believe that women must be full and equal partners in peace negotiations, which is what, we believe, will give these negotiations a fair chance of success.

Who does the negotiating right now? Not unlike the rest of the world, we too have mostly generals sitting at the negotiating table. This is an oxymoron (and sometimes just a moron). We have specialists trained in the art of destroying an enemy, expected to transform themselves into specialists trained in the art of resolving differences amicably. Most mothers would have a head start on almost any general in the art of resolving differences amicably.

This is the message of the Coalition of Women for a Just Peace and of most of the other peace groups (Gush Shalom, the Rabbis for Human Rights, Ta'ayush: Arab-Jewish Partnership, and many other devoted and dedicated groups) whose members are on the streets and in the villages every day of every week trying to dismantle the occupation that is killing us all.

And yet, despite our dedication, we often hit a brick wall—the media. The Israeli media ignore us, and therefore the world media ignore us. Something to do with our message I suspect, something about our message not being the one the government of Israel would like to promote. So with a few brave exceptions the media conveniently, swept up in their sense of duty and patriotism, ignore the voices of dissent as though they do not even exist. Were it not for e-mail and the Internet, where our message thrives and expands, you might not even know about these efforts.

Strikingly our efforts are not marginal inside Israel, despite often being edited out of the media. For example:

- On 29 December 2000, over 3,000 Israeli and Palestinian women marched through the streets of Jerusalem carrying signs that read "End the Occupation" and "We Refuse to be Enemies." We marched right up to those beautiful stone walls of the Old City and draped our message from the ramparts. Can you imagine—in the midst of the violence of the *intifada,* when reportedly everyone hates everyone else—there were thousands of Israeli and Palestinian women marching through Jerusalem carrying proclamations that "We Refuse to be Enemies?" The media ignored us.

- On 4 February, 500 women laid down in a major road in Tel Aviv, holding signs saying "closure," and blocking the entrance to the Israeli Defense Ministry, illustrating to the generals and politicians how it feels to be under closure and not allowed to get to where you are going. Seventeen of us were arrested, accompanied by some rather nasty police behavior, and yet not a word in any newspaper. Incidentally, a small right-wing demonstration the following day, where no one was arrested, was given a lot of publicity.

What explains it? The message. "End the Occupation" is not the message the media want to deliver. I once called up *Ha'aretz,* our liberal newspaper, to ask why they did not take an interest in Women in Black having been nominated for the Nobel Peace Prize. Their response was, "it is not the time for that sort of news."

So what sort of news *is* it the time for? Occupation news? Generals' news? Israeli casualties news? It always seems to be the right time for that.

Now while this feels like a blackout of our message, little by little, over time, and with a great deal of patience and *sumud* (as our Palestinian colleagues say, or hanging in there for the long haul, as I would put it) the Israeli grassroots peace movement has had an impact on Israel's attitudes and policies. One of the main ways we have done it is by affecting key American individuals and institutions. Let me give you three examples:

- Two years ago, when I was on the board of B'Tselem, the human rights organization, we worked with other human rights organizations to get the Israeli Supreme Court to outlaw torture. We accomplished this by getting the deans of prestigious American law schools to speak out against torture. After that, their colleagues and friends on the Supreme Court in Israel could not embarrass themselves in front of their peers by appearing to support torture.

- A law was proposed in the Knesset that would have made it illegal for Israeli Arab organizations to receive funds from Arab organizations outside Israel. The New Israel Fund got members of the U.S. Congress to lobby their friends in the Israeli Knesset, and that law expired in committee.

- In the example most relevant for the current crisis, the Israeli Committee against Home Demolitions dramatically reduced the demolition of Palestinian homes for about a year. Home demolitions were practically halted from the end of the administration of Prime Minister Netanyahu and throughout the entire administration of Prime Minister Ehud Barak. By encouraging American supporters to make massive numbers of direct citizen appeals to the White House and the State Department, the State Department finally issued directives to its embassy in Israel to approach Israeli officials about the demolitions and Clinton raised the issue with Netanyahu. Home demolitions had almost entirely ended before Prime Minister Ariel Sharon came to power, when self-restraint crumbled entirely. A huge number of homes are being demolished again, over 30 in Jerusalem alone this year.

Let me lay it out succinctly as follows: Israel is vulnerable to international pressure, particularly from the U.S. government. You cannot have a friend who gives you almost $3 billion in gifts every year, and not want to stay on that friend's good side. It is that simple. If you cannot stop it, use it as leverage. If and when the United States would exert its influence to push for a just settlement—which European politicians have been doing for some time now, but without the leverage—the Israeli government will have to fall in line.

It is commonly said that Israeli politicians have gone their own way, and you can certainly find individual examples of that, especially in Sharon's recent acts of defiance. Nevertheless, taking the long view you see increased movement toward resolving this conflict, and much of that has come from the outside. Look at how much progress has been made in the ten years since the Madrid Conference. In Madrid, the Israeli delegates ludicrously ignored Chairman Arafat's presence, and today Israelis may not like or respect Arafat, but we deal with him. Recall that it was once illegal for Israelis to meet with the Palestine Liberation Organization (PLO), but today they are considered legitimate representatives of the Palestinian people. There has also been progress on all the specific issues—approval of a Palestinian state, movement on the Jerusalem issue, and people on both sides exploring options to achieve some share of justice for the Palestinian refugees.

And yet much ground has been lost during the current *intifada*. Some of that lost ground is a result of Barak's spin on the Camp David meetings, claiming that he offered Arafat "the moon," and was turned down. His claim has done colossal damage to the belief among Israelis that peace is attainable with Arafat. The other major barrier to peace is Palestinian violence inside Israel. Every time a bomb goes off inside Israel—Jerusalem, Tel-Aviv, or Hadera—the people of Israel harden their hearts against peace. Every Palestinian bomb hands the right-wing government another seat in the Knesset.

But we *can* return to a peace track. We *can* recapture the belief among 80 percent of Israelis that a Palestinian state is inevitable, and that we in Israel can live with it. One major element is rebuilding Israeli faith that peace is the best form of security, and that is part of our job as peace activists. As Jewish-Israeli peace activists, it is also our job to influence the American-Jewish community and we work extensively on that objective. Another element is containing the extremist elements on both sides of the Green Line—a hard job given the lack of will among the current leaders on both sides. But one incredibly important element in the peace equation, in fact the most powerful element at this moment in history, is the willingness of the U.S. government to actually use its considerable leverage. If I could successfully convey one thought to the U.S. government, it would be that there is a large and growing constituency of Jews in America and Israel who do support a just peace in the Middle East and who would applaud American efforts to get there.

America's global needs and the achievement of peace in the Middle East comprise overlapping interests today. This is the moment for the United States to find its voice. Clearly an American view of peace cannot be imposed, but America's silence is more troubling than its words. We in Israel care deeply about what the U.S. government thinks, and the U.S. government is not thinking out loud enough.

I want peace so badly that I can taste it with every breath. I want peace because I love Israel, and this occupation is eating the humanity out of my country. Occupation is destroying the vision we had for our old-new land, destroying the moral fiber of our leaders, and therefore, of our people. Occupation is turning our children into brutal oppressors. It has changed our society from a caring, public-spirited community into a terrified and militaristic population. Occupation is eating our soul, and this does not even begin to describe what the occupation is doing to its obvious victims across the Green Line, the Palestinians.

It is because of our country's desperate need to regain its soul that I appeal to the U.S. government in the name of my colleagues, friends, sisters, and brothers in the large, but unheralded, peace movement of Israel: stop equivocating. Help us bring this horror to an end. Use your power to make peace in the Middle East. The time has come.

Gila Svirsky, an Israeli peace and human rights activist, has been a member of Women in Black since its founding in 1988. She is co-founder of the Coalition of Women for a Just Peace, which has engaged in a number of acts of resistance to end Israel's occupation of the Palestinian territories. She has also been executive director of Bat Shalom and B'Tselem, two leading Israeli organizations advocating an end to human rights abuses and a just solution to the conflict.

Where Do We Go From Here: Palestinian and American Perspectives

Mustafa Barghouthi

President

Union of Palestinian Medical Relief Committees

John Duke Anthony

President

National Council on U.S.-Arab Relations

Where Do We Go from Here?
A Palestinian Perspective

by Mustafa Barghouthi, M.D.

Due to the Israeli closure of the Occupied Territories, Dr. Barghouthi was unable to travel to Washington. This is the edited transcript of remarks he presented via telephone.

MR. SHARABI: Dr. Barghouthi is probably known to most of you. He is the President of the Palestinian Medical Relief Committees, which is one of the largest and most successful non-governmental organizations (NGOs) in the West Bank and Gaza. Last May, when I was in Palestine, he took me with him in his ambulance and showed me what his committee has been doing, fantastic work in clinics, education, cultural and community development. He, along with other prominent Palestinians, is an advocate for the rise of a new Palestinian democratic movement in the West Bank and Gaza. Dr. Barghouthi, welcome to Washington. We have an audience waiting to hear you.

DR. BARGHOUTHI: Thank you so much, Dr. Sharabi. I would like to greet all your audience today, and I would like to thank the Center on Policy Analysis and Dr. Sharabi in particular for giving me this wonderful opportunity to speak to you, even though I cannot be with you now. I am very pleased to be able to talk to you today.

Let me start by explaining to you a little bit about the existing situation in which we live. I am speaking to you from Ramallah, and we are literally surrounded by tanks. Like many other cities of the West Bank, we are under complete siege. The Israeli planes from time to time—Apache helicopters and other kinds of planes—attack civilian cities and still conduct assassinations, a policy that was declared by [Israeli Prime Minister] Mr. Sharon as an official policy that will continue. His statement was made one day after the visit of [British Prime Minister] Mr. Blair, who was trying to establish a new road for some kind of settlement.

During the last 48 hours, eight new assassinations were conducted, bringing the number of illegal assassinations to 71. Out of the 18 percent of the West Bank and the Gaza Strip which is under the Palestinian Authority (PA), almost every city in this area of the West Bank has been invaded by Israeli tanks, which are still present in Ramallah, Nablus, the areas Tulkarem, Jenin, Qalqiya, surrounding Hebron and Jericho and also still surrounding Bethlehem and Beit Jalah, from which they withdrew recently, leaving a huge amount of destruction.

Many neighborhoods in these cities are under curfew. The neighborhoods in Ramallah where there are still tanks have been under curfew for the last fifteen days. What we are witnessing here is something that is unprecedented even in any other previous occupation. What is happening, in addition to incursions and invasions, is a process of collective punishment, where 121 Israeli barricades have transformed the West Bank and the Gaza Strip into 220 clusters of prisons, separated completely from each other.

Just to give you an idea of what I am talking about, there are two little towns—Turmus'ayya and Sinjil—they are both located between Ramallah and Nablus. By the way, many of the people who live in these villages are American citizens. These two villages are very close to each other. The distance between the border of one village and the other is eight meters, literally. Crossing from one village to the other, these eight meters, requires, at the moment, five hours of traveling, simply because the closure that is imposed is cutting the country into pieces and creating a system of ghettos, and a system of discrimination and bantustans, that has never existed anywhere else, not even in South Africa.

We had many delegations that visited us from South Africa, and their main conclusion after their visit was that they have never seen anything like that, even in the worst times of the apartheid system in South Africa. What I want to alert you to is that Mr. Sharon and his government are conducting a systematic process of destruction of the Palestinian infrastructure. What is happening is a systematic process of destruction of everything, of anything that we managed to build during the last seven years. There is a very dangerous process of destruction of the potential of the establishment of a Palestinian state. And thus there is a process that aims at destroying the potential and the possibility of peace and peaceful coexistence that is based on a two state solution.

In the process of this destruction, there has been huge and unacceptable humanitarian loss. We have lost up till now 801 Palestinians who were killed and 190 Israelis, too. Out of the 801 Palestinians who were killed so far, one-third were children. Sixty percent of those killed have never participated, and did not participate, in any kind of anti-Israeli activity, not even peaceful demonstrations. They were killed inside their homes, their schools, their neighborhoods. Ninety-nine percent of them were shot in the upper part of the body, which means they were shot to be killed, and 802 people makes approximately 76,000 people that would have been killed if these incidents had happened in the United States considering the size of population. It is a huge number of victims.

In addition to that, there are 24,000 people who have been injured during this year, 1,500 of them have become permanently disabled. We are talking about almost one percent of the total population of the West Bank, the Gaza Strip, and East Jerusalem that have become either martyrs, injured, or permanently disabled.

In addition to that, this destruction process has cost us 50 percent of the gross domestic product (GDP). There is unemployment that reached about 52 percent, and 62 percent of the total Palestinian population live below the poverty line, which is two dollars per capita per day. What is happening, in my opinion, is a war crime, a war crime that is unacceptable.

To add insult to injury, the most recent act of the Israeli army in Beit Rima—a village that was recently invaded by the Israeli army—left us with a new model that is going to be repeated in other places. It has happened in Araba and Jenin, where the army invaded the village, shot people where there was practically no fight, no resistance. Nobody could resist attacks of Apache helicopters and tanks. In that village, the most terrible thing that happened is that injured people were left to bleed to death, without the Israeli army allowing ambulances to enter the village. For six hours, we were pleading with every international organization to allow ambulances to get to the injured people, and unfortunately these injured people were left to bleed to death.

This, in my opinion, is state terrorism, and it is the worst kind of oppression. The world must realize that Israel cannot continue to behave as it is, as though it has impunity to international law. And the world must ask the question why Israel still insists on refusing to have any kind of international presence on the ground. Is it because Israel does not want the world to know the reality? For the first time maybe in history, what is happening here on the ground is a situation where Israel is combining a military occupation with war that is conducted against a civilian population.

What Sharon is trying to establish is to impose on Palestinians a situation not of cease-fire, but a situation of unilateral cease-fire. What Sharon has been trying to do, he and Netanyahu and people like them, is to separate and divide the world into two pieces. In one piece you have Afghanistan, bin Laden, Iraq, and Palestine, and on the other side you have the United States, the West, and Israel. What Sharon and Netanyahu, by doing so, are trying to do, is to justify an unjustifiable occupation and oppression.

They are exploiting the tragedy that befell the United States. This is a cheap policy and it must not be allowed to continue to justify Israeli violations of international law, and their efforts to sustain an unsustainable military occupation.

What I want to alert you to, is the fact that this Israeli military occupation of the West Bank and the Gaza Strip is becoming the longest occupation in modern history. And the world's realization—especially after the tragedy on 11 September—that their strategic stability in the region and in the world depends on the resolution of the Palestinian-Israeli conflict, provides us with an opportunity to find a solution and a resolution.

But I must say that this opportunity does not provide guarantees. There are no guarantees that this opportunity will be used, and this opportunity may also, therefore, be lost. There is a risk and a danger that Israel will continue with the support of the lobby that supports Israel and that is very powerful in certain structures, like the U.S. Congress, to try to use this power that they have to bypass the possibility of finding a real solution. Their effort is directed at trying to create some kind of situation that provides artificial calm at the expense, not only of

Palestinian rights, but also of the possibility and the potential for a true solution that can provide stability for everybody in this region and for the world.

There is an opportunity that exists, but this opportunity cannot be used unless certain conditions are accepted. I would like to specify four preconditions that, in my opinion, represent or provide the opportunity for a real solution in this place. These are preconditions that I believe the United States must accept if it wants to play a positive role in this region.

The first precondition is that you cannot equate between the two sides. You cannot equate between an occupier and the occupied people. It is unacceptable to ask the Palestinian people not to resist occupation. In my opinion, asking the Palestinian people not to resist occupation is exactly like asking a woman that is being raped not to scream. The world must understand the suffering of the Palestinian people and the suffering of people who have been under occupation for such a long time. If the United States wants to help Israel, it must also help Israel not to feel immunity for the crimes it is committing and the violations it is committing against international law.

I want to alert you to the fact that there is a very serious, dangerous shift in Israel to the right and towards extremism and racism. The most recent poll that was conducted in Israel showed that 50 percent of Israelis support the transfer policy, which is a policy of ethnic cleansing. Seventy percent of those who were asked said that they would support the assassination policy, a policy that is a violation of every international law, and which makes the Israeli government the judge, the jury, and the executioner at the same time. Sixty-six percent of Israelis said they support the incursions and reoccupation of Palestinian cities, and said they support Sharon's rejection of American demands to withdraw from Palestinian cities. In my opinion, Israel has been spoiled by the unconditional American support and the lack of intervention from the international community to force Israel to accept international law. Israel is the only country that does these things, and it must be stopped for the sake, not only of Palestinian children and their futures, but also for the sake of the future of Palestinian, Israeli, and American children.

The second precondition—and allow me to specify it as a doctor who knows that it is a big mistake to be consumed with the symptoms of the disease rather than treating the cause of the disease—is that the world must pay attention, and the United States must pay attention to removing the cause of this conflict. The cause of this conflict has been, and still is, the military occupation of the West Bank, the Gaza Strip, and East Jerusalem. This occupation has become the cancer that is destroying the people in this region and destroying their interests and their future. A solution in this region cannot be achieved without recognition of the right of the Palestinians for freedom, for dignity, for independence, and for democracy.

The third precondition that, I believe, is very important, is that there should be a clear recognition of the historical compromise that was made by the Palestinians and the Palestinian people when they accepted to have a state within the boundaries of the West Bank, the Gaza Strip, and East Jerusalem—which represents only 22 percent of the land of historic Palestine instead of 45 percent which was assigned to Palestinians as a Palestinian state in the partition plan, on the basis of which Israel was established as a state. One cannot compromise the compromise. That is why either there will be a sustainable, democratic, prosperous Palestinian state with a minimum of territory—and that is the West Bank, the Gaza Strip, and East Jerusalem—a state that can be sovereign and can be responsible for the future of its citizens, or we are not talking about a real solution. The right of Palestinians for ending occupation—to guarantee the rights of the refugees, to guarantee their right in Jerusalem, East Jerusalem as their capital, and to guarantee a true, sovereign, and sustainable state—means the removal of illegal Israeli settlements which were established against international law as well.

The fourth, and most important, precondition is that you cannot leave this problem to be resolved only by the two sides. Therefore, the current intervention in the region by the international community will not help. We have lost already ten years since the Madrid Conference was convened, and we have lost seven years in all since the Oslo agreements were signed. This Israeli government, especially this Israeli government headed by Sharon, is not a government that is planning to make peace, or is willing to make peace, or is capable of making peace. There has to be a true international intervention that aims at imposing international law and the application of international resolutions, including the withdrawal of Israeli armies from the Occupied Territories exactly as has happened in the south of Lebanon. An active, strong, international intervention that would provide a balanced international framework for true negotiations that could lead to the implementation of UN resolutions, combined hopefully with some form of international presence and protection, would, in our opinion, allow for the possibility of a sustainable peace in this region.

We as Palestinians have many preconditions to meet as well, including sustaining Palestinian national unity through the consolidation of internal democracy, and not accepting all these pressures that are exercised now on Palestinians to transform the PA into a dictatorship that oppresses its own people. This cannot be allowed to happen, because if it happens, then this will not lead to peace. A true peace, as we have experienced in many other parts of the world, is that peace that can be made only between democracies.

The other aspect that Palestinians must care about is how to continue this struggle, and how we can establish a unified national strategy that cares about what happens on the ground, the ability of people to sustain the terrible pressures that they are encountering, and taking into consideration our ability to gain support in the Arab world and the international arena.

And finally, and we are trying to achieve this, to have a unified and clear political message. I would like to convey what I believe this message is. We as Palestinians want a true and sustainable peace. We want justice and freedom for the Palestinian people. We will not, and I do not believe that the Palestinian people will ever, give up on our right for human dignity and the right to live on an equitable basis with other people. The late, very famous Palestinian poet Tawfiq Zayed once said something that is very important to us. He said that we, the Palestinians, are not better than any other people in this world, but no other people are better than us. We all are the sons and daughters of God, and we all deserve to be treated as equals. Nothing, believe me, nothing—not the bias in the media to Israel, not the killing and the oppression that Palestinians suffer from, and not all these threats that we are encountering—will stop the Palestinians from continuing their struggle for a just and durable peace, for their freedom, and for their dignity. Nothing will break the Palestinian people. We shall continue the struggle for the sake of us and for the sake of you, to achieve freedom, because only then, only then when Palestinians can be free, will the Middle East be a peaceful place, and the world will be a truly peaceful place.

This injustice against the Palestinian people that has lasted for the last 84 years must end. We hope that you will be on our side in this struggle for a real peace, for justice, for freedom, and human dignity. Thank you so much.

MR. SHARABI: Thank you very much, Dr. Barghouthi, for your moving and eloquent words. On behalf of the audience here, we send you and your colleagues, and the Palestinian people in their just struggle, all our best wishes, and some of us, our prayers. We hope to see you at our next meeting in person. Goodbye.

DR. BARGHOUTHI: Thank you, and I hope to see you too, all of you, and best greetings to you from here, from Palestine. Thank you so much.

Mustafa Barghouthi, M.D., is president of the Union of Palestinian Medical Relief Committees, one of the largest and most successful NGOs in the West Bank and Gaza Strip, providing health care and education to people in rural areas. He initiated the NGO network, a non-partisan, multi-sector umbrella group of Palestinian NGOs working to advance democratic practices within the Palestinian Authority. He, along with other prominent Palestinians, is an advocate for the rise of a new Palestinian democratic movement in the West Bank and the Gaza Strip.

Arriving Home:
Thinking 'Out of the Box' on Palestine

by John Duke Anthony

Prior to 1947, America had neither enemies in the Middle East, nor adversaries or critics. In the entire region from Morocco to Muscat, and from Baghdad to Berbera, with Aden, Algeria, and Aleppo in between, its image was the land of the free and the home of the brave.

Sadly, much of the goodwill that had been built up by previous generations of American doctors, nurses, teachers, and business representatives has been drained. There are several reasons. The oldest reason, and by far the most important, is the ongoing region-wide reaction to official American policies and positions related to Palestine.

Should a just, durable, and comprehensive settlement to the Israeli-Palestinian conflict remain elusive, the United States will suffer increasingly heavy blows to its national interests. A prolongation of the conflict will continue to pose outsized threats to Israelis, Palestinians, and Americans alike.

Notwithstanding the denials of numerous pundits and politicians, Israeli and American action and inaction on matters pertaining to Israel and Palestine, as well as Syria, are much more deeply embedded in what has spawned and what sustains terrorism than many recognize.

An auspicious moment

The most auspicious moment for statesmen to exert bold, visionary, and determined leadership on an issue of importance to all of humankind does not occur every day. But now is as fortuitous a juncture for the United States to do so as any since the onset of the Israeli occupation 34 years ago. The goal: to bring one of the longest, most protracted, and dangerous of modern wars to an end.

In the eyes of millions, the present circumstances could not be more favorable, and the setting could not be more propitious. In no previous period have as many Americans been as open-minded, anxious, and willing to learn from the bottom up why America's standing in one of the world's most important regions is untenable and dangerous.

Never before have so many Americans been as oriented toward better understanding the roots of the one issue that, more than any other, is behind the mounting anger and distrust towards the United States: the Arab-Israeli conflict and the U.S. role therein.

Consider the following. Israel's critics refer to the past fifteen years and, with reference to today's "Operation Enduring Freedom," note that Israel is one of the few countries that was not invited to join the U.S.-led coalition. Indeed, this is the third time in succession in a major regional crisis involving U.S.-Middle East relations and interests when Washington, in effect, has informed Israel: "Thanks for your offer of assistance, but no thanks."

The reason: Israel's overt participation would pose strategic liabilities to vital American and Allied needs and concerns in the international effort to stem the tide of terrorism. As many supporters of Israel agree, the fact that Israel's current image is the opposite of what its leaders have long tried to project is more than alarming. Left unattended and uncorrected, the implications for important Israeli interests, including its relationship with the United States, could be devastating.

Charles de Gaulle re-dux

Statesmen of any country with such a widespread international image problem would regard such a situation as ominous, and even more so in this case. Why? Because numerous other countries, including most of the world's 22 Arab and 57 Islamic nations, have responded favorably to Washington's request to suit up as American allies in the current campaign against terrorism.

Israel's current status as a strategic liability, as Israel's friends point out, is a clarion call for damage limitation and image improvement. Israel needs to make its own bold and visionary decision, much as France's Charles de Gaulle did when, in the case of Algeria in 1962, he severed his country's colonial control over other peoples' land and resources.

Failure to do so, Israel's friends agree, will continue to harm near-term Israeli strategic, national security, and related concerns. Lack of success on this front will not come cost-free. It will endanger the legitimate interest in self-preservation for generations of Israelis yet unborn.

Apologists for the United States and Israel doing nothing to change their policies toward the Palestine question argue that either a military or an imposed solution is unthinkable. True, if the question is limited to whether the current Congress, and segments of the Israeli Knesset, would be likely to give favorable consideration to either option.

Regrettably, as several specialists in Congressional and Israeli Knesset affairs have informed this writer, "That's the way it is. It's just not going to happen." In response, one analyst who follows both Israeli and American legislative affairs remarked, "So much for leadership. So much for courage. So much for listening to one's friends, including those in the Israeli peace camp."

Other possibilities

But what about other possibilities? What if the Israeli leadership, on its own initiative, were to decide to cut its losses by ending the illegal occupation and dismantling the settlements? Who can prove to the contrary that such a decision would do more than anything else to help Israel overcome its core difficulty?

Supporters of Israel acknowledge that failure to make such a courageous and far-reaching decision at this time is unlikely to be without consequences: it is hard to envision an eventuality in which there will not at some point be an Allied-choreographed action to impose a solution.

"Either that," said one, "or growing numbers will argue that American taxpayers can no longer afford to proceed as though it is business as usual. How could the United States continue to provide Israel an average of $115 per second, $6,777 per minute, and $10 million a day as it has for the past 20 years?"

Political factors and international support

Currently, virtually all of the world's most important leaders would support President Bush were he to take the lead in bringing this conflict to a close. This includes the overwhelming majority of the member countries of the UN General Assembly, all four of the United States' fellow Permanent UN Security Council Members, and the heads of prominent international organizations in every major region and sub-region. They would do so in order that all parties to the conflict benefit from ending the occupation. Few other measures could be expected, over time, to produce as positive a set of results in support of vital global interests in regional peace and stability.

The timing for such a clear-headed strategic initiative is ripe for two other reasons. One, neither the United States nor Israel is presently weighed down with the dynamics and demands of a major election year. Two, analysts of American elections emphasize that the vast majority of America's more ardent supporters of Israel's continued colonization of Palestinian land raised funds, campaigned, and voted against President Bush.

Optimists posit that there is therefore no credible domestic or international rationale why the President should delay taking appropriate measures to lift the United States and Israel out of their political and national security quagmires. The goal: to free Israel and its American supporters of the overwhelming burden that is tarnishing their reputations in the eyes of the world, eating away at their bodies politic, and dragging them down—morally, financially, politically, nationally, and regionally.

U.S. needs, concerns, interests

Hard-minded strategists agree with this assessment and recommendation, but come at the topic somewhat differently. They note that the United States is currently—and will continue to be until far into the future—in greater need of the friendship, economic, and strategic assistance of key Arab and Islamic countries than it has been in quite some time.

Much of the necessary Arab, Muslim, and Israeli peace camp consensus in support of a bold peace initiative is already in hand. Additional assistance will follow once the United States moves beyond rhetoric to enable Israelis, Palestinians, Syrians, Americans, and others to be rid of this long soul-wrenching nightmare.

How? By ending the occupation and the settlements and, thereby, the principal threats to Israel's national security and regional standing, and the injustice and indignities visited upon the Palestinians and Syrians since Israel seized their territories in 1967.

The straight talk express?

It is a given that some will insist now is not a good time, or now is the worst possible time, to end the occupation. Their arguments will echo the leaders of previous colonial powers who contended that to do so "would be tantamount to appeasement; it would only reward terrorism." "A bloodbath would ensue." "All hell would break loose."

Assertions such as these make for good copy, but they are mere surmise and conjecture. What is indisputable is that few, if any, colonial powers have ever found it easy or convenient to relinquish control over the countries whose lands they had colonized. One must never underestimate the tenacity of those who favor the *status quo.* The prolongation of power, the perpetuation of privilege, has always been addictive.

Even so, in the century just past, a dozen colonial powers conceded to their subject peoples the right to freedom and independence. In each instance, colonizer and colonized alike emerged and have remained by far the freer, better, and stronger.

Many wonder whether there can be any serious doubt that it is only a matter of time before something of the same will be the fate of Israel's illegal colonial outposts in Palestine and Syria. Others agree and doubt whether the nature and extent of violence between Israelis and Palestinians as well as Syrians, and against Americans and U.S. interests, can be expected to cease otherwise.

If not, the question will be at what cost to Israelis, Arabs, Americans, and others for Israel not ending the occupation? And how many more Arab, American, Israeli—and how many more Christian, Jewish, Muslim—and other orphans, widows, widowers, and the maimed, whose dreams will have been destroyed forever, must there be?

Facts are stubborn things

It has been ten years since an American President enjoyed such vast domestic approval in response to his statements on the Palestine question. Millions of Americans, Arabs, and Israelis—millions of Christians, Jews, and Muslims—agree that, in his remarks on this issue to the American people since 11 September, the President has made much sense.

Indeed, the President has stated more positive and factual things about America's Arab and Islamic friends, allies, and strategic partners, and about the beliefs, practices, and institutions of the Muslim faith, than all previous American presidents combined.

And most importantly, President Bush, Great Britain's Prime Minister Tony Blair, and other world leaders have proclaimed support for the establishment of a Palestinian state. In response, few specialists are surprised at the reaction among some segments of the American public.

The media and some members of Congress have mounted a smear campaign in opposition to the President's positions. Without citing him by name, critics contest his upbeat depiction of Arabs and Muslims in general, and of America's vital interests in the 22 Arab states and the 57 countries that comprise the Islamic world.

Cynics and pessimists hold that the arguments in support of an American move toward more decisive engagement in ending the Arab-Israeli dispute are irresponsible and dangerous. Such assertions are mere surmise and conjecture. Taking such steps at this time would benefit Americans, Israelis, Palestinians, and Syrians greatly; they would neither betray nor damage the legitimacy of any country or people.

The current effort of hard-line Israeli leaders and their American counterparts to remove such an option from the diplomatic and geopolitical table, and to drive wedges between the United States and key Arab and Islamic countries, is hardly new.

Previous pro-Israel campaigns aimed at bashing Arab and Islamic countries succeeded in getting the United States to lash out at Libya and Lebanon, bomb Baghdad, punish Pakistan, threaten Tehran, and slap sanctions on Sudan and Syria. The focus of the current campaign is different. In addition to the Palestinians and Syrians, it is directed mainly at Egypt and Saudi Arabia, America's two most important Arab allies. And, irony of ironies, the tone, tenor, and targets of such hostile and often inaccurate commentary closely resemble remarks attributed to

Osama bin Laden and other members of his *al-Qaeda* network.

Linkages

Even so, the strong political linkage between the unresolved Palestinian problem on the one hand, and American relations and interests in Egypt, Saudi Arabia, and elsewhere in the Middle East on the other, is undeniable. Ignorance of such realities has no redeeming qualities.

Indeed, it is the implications of the linkage for American interests and policies—for example, in the pressing need to find an early and efficacious way out of the Israeli-Palestinian impasse—that most concerns critics of the United States' special relationships with key Arab and Islamic countries. It is as though opponents of these long-standing and mutually beneficial ties would insist that Washington officialdom limit itself to but one Middle Eastern friend, and that such a friend must be neither Arab nor Muslim.

Every Arab and Muslim knows this. So does every American diplomat, armed forces commander, and corporate representative residing and working in the region. All acknowledge that the ongoing dismay at U.S. policies toward the Palestine problem remains the main impediment to the cause of projecting and protecting America's vital Middle Eastern interests, and to pursuing key U.S. foreign policies in the region as a whole.

In reaffirming his Constitutional duty to defend the United States and the lives of its citizens, President Bush has repeatedly said that he "will take whatever steps are necessary to protect American lives and the interests of the United States." On the face of it, this is reassuring to many, for were he not to do so, Americans at home and abroad would be placed in harm's way even more than they are already.

Essential: A viable independent palestine

For numerous American strategists, and for many decision-makers in the region as well, the President's announcement in favor of the establishment of a Palestinian state was timely and essential. Needed now is an American commitment, a timeline, a detailed plan, and an additional allied coalition to help bring the new state into being.

Such a plan needs to be carefully calibrated and choreographed with key regional leaders and their counterparts among the major powers. To this end, members of the Committee for the Nobel Prize for Peace and the International Court of Justice might be asked to serve as observers and supervisors to ensure that the plan is implemented, and to vouchsafe for the integrity of the process.

Why the urgent necessity of effective early movement and leadership on this issue? Because the occupation continues to fuel most of the violence between Arabs and Israelis. Because the increasing hatred of the United States for its *de facto* support of the occupation carries its own clear and present danger to Americans and important American interests. Because much of the regional anger against America remains deeply rooted in Washington's role in shielding Israel from international censure, responsibility, and accountability for its failure to end the occupation.

Ending an era and an error

Now is also the time to start putting into place the economic, social, and humanitarian assistance, along with the requisite infrastructure measures, that are essential to ensuring a viable Palestinian state is brought into being as soon as possible. Combined with the reality of an end to the occupation, no other act would do more to help restore American goodwill and, en route to a brighter future for all parties to the conflict, push the memory of the Holocaust's horrors and the unending trauma of Palestinian and Syrian dispossession, farther back into the recesses of history.

An expeditious and effective end to the occupation is also necessary in order to sow the seeds for the peace and security that has eluded Israel and to end the systematic subjugation that has robbed Palestinians and Syrians of their freedom, dignity, and elemental human rights since the occupation began.

The moral and policy imperatives of establishing such a state, many are convinced, are linked directly to vital American strategic requirements and national security interests. For this reason, the initiative needs to become part and parcel of the broader effort by the United States and its allies against the roots, staying power, and manifestations of terrorism.

The decision to act decisively now will not be synonymous with appeasement. It is nothing of the kind. The rationale for taking such action at this time is to end an era and an error, to right a wrong, to protect American and allied lives and livelihoods that are linked to the United States' relationship with Israel and many other countries in the region. By doing so, the United States will ascend to the moral, political, and strategic high ground. It will have done the right thing, at the right time, in the right way, for the right reasons.

Out of harm's way

On the defense front, the following is revealing. None of the commanders-in-chief of U.S. Central Command (CENTCOM), the forward deployed force tasked with promoting and protecting American and allied interests in the region since 1979, has failed to inform American policymakers of the most pervasive and persistent threat to American regional relations and interests.

The commanders have regularly shared with Washington, and this analyst, what their more than two dozen governmental counterparts in CENTCOM's area of responsibility—and especially in Egypt, Jordan, and the Gulf region—have had to say in opposition to American policies. The near unanimous view of these allied leaders is that U.S. policy toward the Palestine question has, in effect, prevented the people of Palestine from being free in their own land and have, thereby, contributed directly to much of the regional instability that Bush Administration officials, and their predecessors, have repeatedly professed it is in America's vital interest to end. What is more, these leaders have consistently underscored the CENTCOM host countries' perception that the United States is the main reason for the continued Israeli occupation.

If one message is more urgent than others, on which the leaders of all of America's Arab and Muslim allies—and many in the Israeli peace camp—agree, it is that once Israel's occupation of Arab lands has ended, no one need trumpet the obvious: Palestinians, Syrians, and Israelis, as a direct result, will be far along the road to being free.

Palestinians will at least, and at last, be free to become a country. Syrians will be free of foreign occupation of one of their country's most resource-rich provinces. Israelis will be free in a different way: they will have had lifted from their shoulders one of their heaviest and costliest burdens.

Major steps will have been taken in the campaign against the most unending source of Middle East-based terrorism and in the quest to enhance the acceptability and respectability of the United States—and of Israelis, Palestinians, and Syrians—in the region as a whole.

Not a panacea, but far more than a palliative

Ending the occupation and the settlements will not eradicate political violence. Neither will it eliminate all of the sources of terrorism in the Middle East and elsewhere. However, like nothing else, it will bring to Americans, Israelis, Palestinians, and Syrians alike a far greater measure of personal, institutional, and national security than they have attained since the onset of Israel's occupation.

A speedy end to the occupation will remove the single oldest, largest, and most pervasive phenomenon that underlies much of the Arab Christian and Islamic anger against Israelis and Americans. It will do much to help pave the way for eventual Arab-Israeli reconciliation. It will put into place the stepping stone to ending Israeli insecurity and isolation from its neighbors, and to ending Palestinian and Syrian insecurity and misery. Without such a step it is difficult to envision Israel, Palestine, and Syria being able to establish and sustain peaceful and reciprocally rewarding relationships with other countries in the region.

U.S. strategic needs

In all of this, the United States' strategic objective is manifold. In its most elemental aspects the objective is to place America's relations with the entire region on as positive, secure, and stable a foundation as possible. The requisite vision for achieving such an objective needs to be focused on securing the legitimate interests of the region's member states in their longing to be away from war and threats to peace.

Such a vision also needs to be focused on ensuring the basic economic interests of the region as well as the outside world. For both, these encompass unfettered access to the region's prodigious energy resources in adequate supplies and at manageable prices.

The vision, moreover, needs to be focused on assuring broad political interests. In more peaceful and stable circumstances than currently prevail, these would ordinarily flow from the proclamation and administration of the Middle East countries' moderate foreign policies and interstate relations in accordance with the precepts of the UN Charter, UN Security Council resolutions, and other norms of international law and legitimacy.

In addition, the vision needs to allow for a robust commercial environment. Such an environment would enable and provide protection for steadily increasing levels of trade, investment, and joint business ventures. And the vision needs to be focused on providing jointly determined and effective arrangements for defending the member states' legitimate rights to self-preservation and against any threats to their national sovereignty, political independence, and territorial integrity.

Curtain call

At the end of the day, reality brooks no illusions. This, after all, is the twenty-first century. The idea that any country receiving official American support should be allowed to continue its occupation and colonization of another has few, if any, credible backers.

The road toward freedom, peace, security, and stability for Arabs and Israelis, two proud and historic peoples, will not be easy. Such things never are. But in getting from here to there, one need not agree with the cynics. The latter would have one believe that the two peoples and their supporters are irreversibly locked into a downward spiral that is headed towards a clash between their respective cultures and civilizations.

The reality is the opposite. In contrast to those who insist upon seeing either of the two sides and their primary supporters in this conflict as "those," as "them," as "other," one need only ponder the following.

Not "other-ness, " but "us-ness"

Among Christians, Jews, and Muslims—and among Arabs, Israelis, and millions of Americans too—there still flickers an age-old, special sense of "us-ness." One would do well to reconsider the implications of this "us-ness" in terms of what remains to be achieved in ending the occupation and dismantling the settlements in the days to come.

Here in this region of current and seemingly constant conflict and tension, as in no other single place on earth, is the crucible of culture, the cradle of civilization, the anvil of antiquity, the nursery of nations, the source of sunshine on the classical world. Here too is the crossroads of three continents and the birthplace of the world's three monotheistic religions.

The combination of these attributes has the effect of making the entire region sometimes seem as though it were one big traffic jam of the devout. That and something else: namely, the epicenter of prayer and pilgrimage, of faith and spiritual devotion, for more than half of humanity.

In pointing the way forward, this much seems clear: it is way past time for all the parties to this conflict to leave the battlefield and come home. Germany and France, Russia and Central Europe, Canada and Great Britain, have no patent on the process, no monopoly on the technique, of turning swords into plowshares. In this instance, the United States cannot afford to be seen to be asleep at the wheel.

Moral courage

America's Arab and Islamic partners and those in the Israeli peace camp rightly argue that the United States will do Americans, Arabs, and Israelis no favor should it refuse to assume the mantle of responsibility, accountability, and courage—of political, personal, physical, and above all, moral courage—that it has long urged upon others.

If one is serious about supporting and defending the legitimate rights of Americans, Israelis, Palestinians, Syrians, and many others, there would appear to be no alternative to moving as quickly as possible toward achieving the strategic and related objectives outlined here.

Saying that one will do whatever is necessary to make headway in the struggle against the causes and manifestations of terrorism in the name of protecting American lives and advancing vital American national interests is commendable. However, in pursuit of such laudable goals, it is hard to see how refusal or failure to end the illegal Israeli occupation—together with the equally illegal settlements that the occupation has spurred and to this day sustains—could be a winning strategy and policy option.

To paraphrase Edmund Burke, all that is necessary for systematic and institutionalized suppression and injustice to prevail, and in this case, for relentless anger and acts of terror against Americans, Arabs, and Israelis to continue, is that enough good people do nothing.

 *John Duke Anthony is president and CEO of the National Council on U.S.-Arab Relations; secretary, U.S.-GCC Corporate Cooperation Committee; and publisher,* Gulf Wire. *All three are non-profit NGOs dedicated to educating Americans and others of U.S. interests and involvement in the Arab countries, the Middle East, and the Islamic world.*